Odin's Last Rune

A Fascinating English Journey

Odin's Last Rune

Blisters, Battles and Beliefs
on the Coast-to-Coast Walk

Almis Simankevicius

GOOD WALKING
BOOKS

Odin's Last Rune

Published by GoodWalking Books
PO Box 1112 North Sydney NSW 2060
email: goodwalking@aol.com

ISBN 0-9578968-0-8

Cover art drawn by Lukas Maximas.
Additional illustration by Lukas Maximas and Mikolas Ray.
Maps and photographs by the author.
Book design by RedBanana.
www.redbanana.com.au

Printed and bound by
Southwood Press, Marrickville, NSW 2204, Australia.

Other books in the GoodWalking Books series:
Santiago - Walking the Pilgrim Path.

Contents

Foreword

Familiar names like St. Bees, Ennerdale Bridge and Robin Hood's Bay woke up the sleeping giant in my memory.

I recalled the early days at school, of learning the Norse legends and early English history. After leaving England in 1966, my first return to the country was in 1997, where I showed my Australian wife the locations that I knew about, that had made the history books.

Standing at the base of the remaining city walls in Southampton I imagined the invaders "from across the sea" trying to take the city, then on to London and the North.

My walking adventures in the Boy Scouts were with a pack on my back, through the countryside to many locations which had been written into history or folklore, and of course the obligatory blisters.

Almis has successfully re-ignited those memories with his latest walk "Coast to Coast".

Where will he go next? Whose memory will be rekindled? Will it be the luck of the Irish?

Tom Hunter
April 2001

For

Carol - my partner in this journey

and many thanks to

Lukas and Miki for their graphic visualisations
Min for his editorial and graphic input
Juliet - her enthusiasm and literary support
Tom Hunter
Warwick for his support
Kirstin for her marketing ideas
and to writers such as Nicholas Crane,
A. Wainwright and
many others who have successfully combined
a love of walking with the written word.

⊕

Simankevicius, Almis, 1954- .
Odin's Last Rune.

Bibliography.
Includes index.
ISBN 0 9578968 0 8.

1. Walking - England. 2. Mythology, Norse. 3. Middle Ages - History.
4. England - Description and travel. I. Title.

914.2

The Runes Themselves:

Runes are the symbols which make up the alphabet used by the Anglo-Saxon, Norse and Germanic peoples from around 1,500 years ago.

They are also a magical and divinatory system.

RAD - travel or journey

GYFU - a gift

ANSUR - prophecy or revelation

IS - freezing

EHWAZ - progress

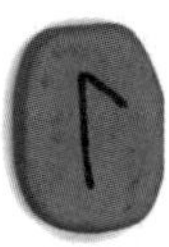

LAGU - water

THORN - boundless energy

HAGAL - elemental disruption

GER - harvest of past actions

EOH - evergreen, death

BEORC - purification, renewal

The book weaves together...

three strands of writing:
- the mythological
- the historical
- a contemporary journey across England.

A rune and its meaning begin each chapter of the myths, while the historical chapters have a date included in their headings.

The chapters that describe the journey itself have this symbol along the chapter's heading: ⊕

Distances from St Bees
in Miles

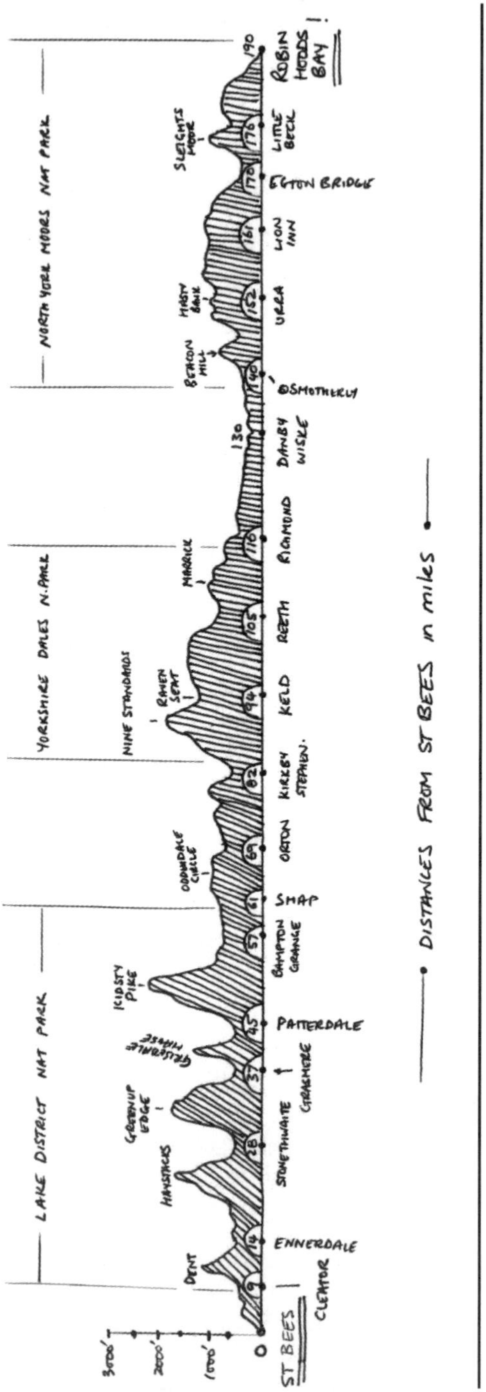

Odin
The Allfather

RAD
(the journey)

Amongst the icy wastes of the earth's northern reaches, bitter winds scoured and scraped the frozen tundra as they had done for millennia. In this desolate emptiness, a solitary fur-clad figure, circled by two ravens, crunched his way across the twisted terrain of ice. A blinding sun reflected from the countless ice crystals that covered the incredibly white landscape. Jagged outcrops of dark rocks draped with glassy capes punctured the fields of impossibly thick ice. Harsh winds sheared razor sharp slivers from the heavy icicles, and whizzed them through the cold air in streams of tiny arrows.

With a thin cord slung around a shoulder and a lustrous golden dagger tucked into his belt, the solidly built man made his way towards the only other living thing in sight - a gigantic ash tree. Strangely coloured leaves adorned the branches of the immense tree, which reached up into the distant skies; its roots lost in the depths of the earth. Incessant winds howled around the tree, causing the fluorescent foliage to flex and shimmer in the relentless light.

The powerful figure stopped in front of the monstrous ash and looked up at it. Such splendour, so much power and mystery he recognized in the tree. This was Yggdrasil, the Tree of Life, which connected heaven and earth. He stood, awed by the ash, mesmerized by its magnificence.

He announced himself to Yggdrasil, shouting to hear himself above the roar of the wind.

"Tree of the heavens, tree of the world, I come to perform this ritual upon your mighty boughs. Support me as you have supported the sky and the earth since time began."

Removing the thin cord from around his shoulder, he tied the heavy golden dagger to one end. With his mighty arm he threw the dagger up and over a thick branch, letting it fall back to the ground. He untied the dagger and clenched it between his teeth. Fashioning a noose from the other end of the cord he slipped it over his head and tightened it around his neck. He grabbed the loose end of the cord and began to hoist himself up, effectively hanging himself. Once his feet were some distance off the ground he secured the loose end around the massive tree's girth.

He withdrew the dagger from between his clenched teeth and clasping it with both hands, pierced his heart till his powers began to drain away. His head slumped back while the blood stained dagger slipped from his tremulous hands and dropped onto the icy ground where it lay alongside the crimson pools of rapidly cooling blood.The winds rose again, and the light of the day was replaced by an unimaginable darkness.

Odin hung heavily on this mysterious tree as the winds shrieked and buffeted him and the razor sharp ice slivers punctured his body. Odin, the Allfather, mighty chieftain of the gods, the god of the occult, patron of magicians and warriors, was at the mercy of his own action. The two ravens settled themselves on one of the inner branches away from the force of the wind and waited...

* * *

This mysterious ash tree grew in the mystical centre of Asgard - the home of the gods, where Odin reigned, accompanied by his two jet-black ravens - Mind and Memory, who usually perched on his shoulders, keeping him informed of all that happened.

There were the other gods as well. Frigg, Odin's wife and the mother of his sons, was the goddess of the earth. The first son, Thor the Thunderer was the patron god of seamen and farmers. He was the god of the sky, ruler of storms and wielder of thunderbolts. Thor was the protector of the universe, guarding the world from the menace of the giants who lived just outside civilization. He had a mighty hammer, which he often brandished about and always carried with him to deal with any frost or mountain giants he encountered. Sometimes the giants outwitted Thor, but he usually triumphed in the end. Thor travelled in a chariot drawn by two magic goats. He was a violent but benevolent god and people felt closer to him than to Odin, because Thor was more like them, not distant like the Allfather.

Odin's second son was Balder, the god of light, the most loved of all gods. He was gentle and had a temperament that all liked. Balder's twin brother was blind Hoder, the god of the dark, and Odin's youngest son was brave Hermod who was fleet of foot and possessed an abundance of courage.

As well as Odin's sons there were the twin gods of fecundity, Frey and his voluptuously wanton sister Freya. These twins controlled the rain and sunshine and were responsible for fertility upon the earth.

Another god was Tew, the god of war, who was always busy with martial projects involving men on earth and was the one who did the fighting. Tew being the god of justice, fair law and regulation was renowned for his fearlessness. Odin, himself, rarely fought. He was more of a tactician, who used any available resource for victory.

In Asgard there was a fabulous palace called Valholl, to which Odin's daughters, known as the attractive and seductive Valkyries, would escort slain warriors. Here, the dead warriors were brought back to life to indulge in fierce battles and then feast at nights, having all their wounds healed as they slept.

* * *

As Odin clung to what was left of his life that night, buffeted by the stinging winds, he reminded himself why he was hanging at the end of a branch with his heart pierced. Although he was the chief of the gods, he was also part of the finite world, governed by Orlog - the universal law and as such, had a quest to fulfill.

Men of the northern realms of the earth had made a dark, mystical, sacrificial cult of him, calling on him to help them to victory in their wars against others, tearing flesh apart to win battles. Whole armies of enslaved men were sacrificed to him.

Odin was also the god of poetry and wisdom. Mankind needed these too, in order to live and grow.

His quest was to acquire wisdom and knowledge. So far, he had spent much of his time travelling and gathering knowledge from all he met. He hungered for learning so much that his search seemed never ending.

This self-sacrifice was the next step in his search, and by hanging on the Tree of Life for nine nights he would learn the occult arts and understand the secret alphabet of the runes. And to do this he had to be open of heart and lighter than air. In his brutal way, Odin had managed to achieve this state of being.

⊕ The Catalyst

One rainy Saturday afternoon I found myself in the local library. This large contemporary citadel of information and knowledge attracted all kinds of seekers, enthusiasts, students and pensioners enjoying an unhurried perusal of daily newspapers. Oriental patterned carpets covered the extensive floor space, which, together with the maze of wooden shelves crammed with books, lent the interior an exotic ambience.

The comprehensive travel section, containing commercial travel guides and personal accounts of fascinating global journeys, held a singular attraction for me. As I scanned these shelves a book fell into my hands. On its distinctive red and white dust jacket was a simple map of a route extending across England from the Irish Sea to the North Sea.

The book was Alfred Wainwright's pictorial guide to the Coast to Coast Walk. I flicked through the pages, marvelling at the hand drawn landscape sketches and intrigued by the unusual place names; Keld, Kirkby Stephen and St Bees.

Moving from west to east, the walk crossed the Lake District, the Yorkshire Dales and the North York Moors, from St Bees in the west to Robin Hood's Bay in the east. The combined effect of all this was to re-awaken that interior denizen who dwells within many of us - the Travel Bug. Having been awoken, the Bug prompted me to think, "one day I'll walk that path."

Alfred Wainwright was a celebrated British fell (hill) walker who had written a number of guidebooks in the 1970s. They combined a personable writing style with meticulous sketches. Since then his guidebook "A Coast to Coast Walk" has been eagerly read by walkers and become a classic travel book.

I found the book fascinating and I waited for the opportunity to do the walk with my partner, Carol. Researching the walk and the history of the areas we would cross, took some time, and before we knew it the "day" arrived.

We would begin our walk in the pleasant seaside town of St Bees, situated in Cumbria on the edge of the Irish Sea, then trace an easterly path across northern England to eventually meet the North Sea at an old village called Robin Hood's Bay.

Early spring seemed the best time of the year to walk the route. It would still be slightly chilly with fewer fellow walkers, making accommodation easier to find. Also, spring was the season of renewal after the harsh winter months, so walking across a terrain of emergent growth and catching glimpses of the animal kingdom returning from its annual hibernation was an attractive proposition. We figured that 18 days on the journey would give us sufficient time to soak up the beauty of the landscape and the history and character of this part of England. Over the next few months I saw a number of articles about the Coast to Coast Walk in the travel sections of various magazines and newspapers. As well as impressing us with the marvellous scenery and experiences that awaited the aspiring walker, the articles also warned about wet weather and the hazards of low visibility, especially

The Coast-to-Coast route

on the moors and high fells.

We discovered through our background reading that this route had a rich history, especially the time between the departure of the Roman legions from Britain and the arrival of the Normans, when waves of new continental invaders assaulted Britain. This period from around 400-1066AD, was known as the "Dark Ages".

I found it fascinating to notice and be aware of the legacies of Teutonic and Nordic mythology brought over by the early invaders. These myths and beliefs shaped the history and culture of the land and in due course became an integral part of English life.

The Coast to Coast Walk would take us 190 miles across the landscape of northern England, rich in folklore and history; over lands invaded and settled by Romans, Anglo-Saxons, Vikings and Normans. We were to discover that the further we journeyed along the route, the more we would experience Germanic and Scandinavian influences and legacies. Our journey would become entwined with an ancient terrain, stone villages, myths and past events.

BC 55
Roman occupation

As Julius Caesar observed the misty land across the water, he tightened his cuirass and wrapped his military cape around him. The temperature had dropped noticeably and the strong wind had changed direction.

"By Fortuna, the winds are with us!" exclaimed Caesar. Now that the conditions were favourable, he gave the signal for the commencement of the invasion fleet to cross the broad channel of water.

Caesar was invading the island to extend Rome's dominion over the known world as well as assuring his own dignitas. He intended to bring the island's profitable trade in lead and tin under Roman control. The landing on the foreign shore was difficult and the subsequent skirmishes with the native tribes were bloody. However, events closer to Rome prevented Caesar from completing his ambition and he returned to the Eternal City.

It was a full 98 years later that the Romans sent a large invasion army to this island they called Britannia. In 43AD the newly proclaimed emperor Claudius, chose this military gambit as a gesture to secure his hold on power in Rome. His invasion fleet landed and the disciplined army proceeded to establish military bases from which they began to subdue the province of Britannia. There were continuing confrontations with many of the existing Celtic peoples such as the Cumbrii and Brigantes. Generally, the Romans preferred to make alliances with the tribes and confer upon them the position of "Client Kings" allowing them a measure of self-government.

The Latin invaders began the massive undertaking of building an infrastructure of roads as they moved across the newly conquered land. The road system was a high priority in every Roman conquest as the roads allowed military forces to move quickly. Eventually around 6000 miles of highways were built across the length and breadth of Britannia.

The main highways consisted of the Fosse Road from Bath to Lincoln, Watling Street from London to Chester and Dere Street from Lincoln to the north.

In the north of the country the Romans took over a cleared spot in the forest and built a fort at Eboracum (later known as York). By 69AD the continuing revolts and attacks from the local Brigantes made it necessary for Eboracum to become the hub of Roman activities in northern Britannia. Thus Eboracum in the north joined Londinium (London) and Camolodunum (Colchester) in the South, as a major Roman centre. The warring Picts, a fierce race from the north of the island, were too much trouble for the Latin occupiers so the Roman emperor, Hadrian, erected a massive long stone barrier (Hadrian's Wall) to keep them out of Roman territory.

Eboracum was favoured due to its large civilian population, known as Romano-Britons, and it became the choice of residence for numbers of Roman governors. In 306 while campaigning in Britannia, Constantius Chlorus, the senior Caesar of the west, died and his son Constantine was proclaimed emperor of the Western Roman Empire in the military fort at Eboracum. There were rival claimants for the emperor's seat, which embroiled Constantine in various battles. On the eve of a major battle with one such rival, Maxentius, Constantine had a vision, which convinced him of his direction. In his vision, he saw a Christian symbol emblazoned on all his soldiers' shields. He won this crucial battle and established rule over the entire empire. He took it upon himself to make Christianity the official religion and stopped persecutions of Christians. In Britannia, this new faith gradually mingled with the existing Roman and Celtic religions.

The Romans had their hands full maintaining control over the province.

The fierce Picts took every opportunity to harass them. As well, longhaired Teutonic tribes from the continent were making exploratory raids on Britannia's coastal settlements and many native British tribes were still opposing Roman rule.

⊕ St Bees

The passengers appreciated the relative warmth inside the train's carriage as it lurched forward along the narrow railway line. Carol and I were on board the train from Carlisle to St Bees. To get here, we had flown from Australia to London and taken a train to the city of Carlisle in Cumbria, northwest England. Outside, gusty showers of rain further darkened the already bleak weather. The train line followed the Cumbrian plain past grey industrial settlements incongruously sited amongst wet green fields, as the dull skein of the Irish Sea merged with the indistinct sky.

The train rambled past Whitehaven, a large shipping port and then edging its way around the cliffs, turned inland and came to a brief halt at St Bees. Since the miserable weather had already forced us to don our goretex rainwear, we were prepared for the intermittent rain as we stepped out onto the cold, wet platform. This was English weather after all. No surprise.

Stonehouse Farm, where a pleasant welcome awaited us, was just a short walk from the railway station. The farm was our first night's accommodation and an excellent opportunity to sample an English Bed and Breakfast (B&B). The compact double storied cottage belied a substantial interior. Our room was self-contained with en-suite, central heating and tea-making facilities. After being suitably impressed with the comforts of Stonehouse Farm, it was time for a look around St Bees.

St Bees was named after St Bega, a nun who ministered in Cumbria during the Dark Ages. According to legend, Bega, a young Irish princess, fled her homeland to avoid marrying a Norse king. In those days, the Norse were harassing the coastal settlements of Ireland, England and Scotland. Bega's father had promised her to the Norse king to ensure some protection from further Viking incursions.

But the beautiful, headstrong Bega had plans of a more religious nature. She wanted to serve God as a nun. She fled Ireland and landed on the Cumbrian coast. After a number of adventures, she was received by Lady Egremont and taken to see her husband, a wealthy landowner. Bega asked him for some land on which to build a nunnery. Lord Egremont jokingly replied that he would donate to her all the land that was covered by snow on next midsummer's day.

A few months passed. On the morning of midsummer's day, black clouds from the sea rolled in and it began to snow. During that day it snowed for several miles around, and Bega had her land.

The rain started to fall again, so to escape the damp afternoon we decided to grab a meal at The Queens Hotel, an atmospheric inn on the quiet main street. Inside, the rich smell of roast meats mingled with the yeasty odour of beer, a welcome invitation to two travellers on such an inclement day. There were quite a few people enjoying this convivial Saturday afternoon. I spied a group of walkers drinking their pints and examining a clutter of maps for what I assumed was their coast to coast walk, and introduced Carol and myself as new starters on the walk.

"This time we're only doing a short three-day coastal walk," the tall one said, "Four years ago we did the complete Wainwright's walk and thoroughly enjoyed it, so we're back."

"We keep hearing how wet the walk is. It really can't be that bad?" Carol asked.

"Well, it rained for 12 out of 13 days and there were plenty of bogs. I hope you've brought your compass to help get you through the fogs and mists," one woman cautioned.

I reached for my pocket instinctively. My compass was safely tucked inside. "How hard was it to walk in 13 days?" I wanted to know.

"It was certainly a stretch to cover the distance. The Lake District was hard but mind you, extremely well worth the trouble, though the mist and rain became a serious nuisance," the tall one said.

"Even just to experience the moors is an enlightenment. They have this uncanny lonely and very empty feel to them," added his companion.

"A lot of people manage it in 13 to 15 days," the tall one confirmed, "and you'll find it an absolute delight when you finally make it to the other side."

We didn't mention to the group that we were planning to take a leisurely 18 days.

* * *

Sunday morning and surprise, not a cloud in the sky! Maybe we would have one dry weather day after all. I counted my blessings and prepared myself for an incredible breakfast.

A full English breakfast, which constituted the second most important part of the classic B&B, was a sight to behold. First, a selection of cereals with fruit and yoghurt. This normally filled me up but there it was, just a refreshing teaser for what was to follow. In came the cooked breakfast: two eggs, rashers of bacon, enormous sausages, grilled tomatoes, baked beans, mushrooms in butter and layers of fried bread. To finish off any chance of us leaving the table malnourished, racks of toasted bread, butter, a selection of jams, marmalades and a large pot of tea were brought in. This grand breakfast is OK for walkers, but don't try it at home if you're the sedentary type.

After breakfast I braced myself for the weight of my pack but found it manageable. Carol had organised with a company who had pre-booked our accommodation to have her pack delivered to each night's stay, which meant she had the pleasure of carrying only a day-pack.

We began our walking adventure by striding out onto the main road. Across the fields, the spire of the Church of St Mary and St Bega was clearly visible. The sun had dried much of yesterday's wetness though numerous puddles pockmarked the footpaths. I pushed open the gate to the church grounds. The church itself was constructed from wonderful red sandstone, which appeared to be a common building material in the area. An imposing Norman arch framed the entrance to the church. Solid wooden doors studded with metal bolts, opened to permit entrance. Opposite the Norman arch there was a stone lintel engraved with the figure of a Viking in a boat hooking a large sea creature. The sight fascinated me. This was the first example of Nordic presence on our journey.

Sunday morning service was about to start, so we decided to join in. Afterwards we were invited to stay for coffee and biscuits.

"We could tell that you were starting out today - you look so look clean," chirped Mary who was on coffee duty, as we munched on our biscuits and enjoyed

The form was to dip the toe of one's boot into the salt water to mark the beginning of the walk

the coffee. I was amazed that I still had room left in my stomach after the enormous breakfast.

John, the town's historian, told us that the church was a sister church of St Mary's in York.

"I love the red colour of the sandstone. Is it local?" I asked.

"Yes it is. Some of it was even shipped to America where it was used in the construction of some of the early American government buildings" John said. "In the 1800s, the nearby town of Whitehaven was the largest English sea port on the Atlantic. Rum, sugar and even slaves were transported between England, America and the West Indies. The red sandstone served as ballast in ships leaving the English port," he told us.

After coffee we bade our new friends goodbye and left through the church's lych gate. The fresh wind blew in our faces as we walked along the asphalt road towards the Irish Sea. I realised that I had forgotten to ask John about the significance of the Viking stone work. Once at the seashore, the custom was to dip one's boot into the salt water and so mark the beginning of the walk.

In another account of St Bega's legend, Melvyn Bragg describes Bega's arrival and her subsequent adventures in his book, "Credo". According to Bragg, Bega and her tutor, Padraic, were forced to flee from Ireland because of Bega's refusal to marry an Irish noble. They made their way to this Cumbrian shore and were left stranded here. Bega became very ill so they found a cave in the cliffs and sheltered there for a few days till she was well enough to continue travelling.

As I marvelled at these high cliffs, I wondered which was the cave Bega and Padraic had sheltered in.

The sun was bright and could have warmed the day, but a sharp wind moderated the temperature. The screeching of the seagulls accentuated the coastal atmosphere and I was glad to be walking again. On the map, the walk around St Bees Head seemed quite straightforward, but actually entailed many ascents and descents. It wasn't as easy as the flat map suggested, but the marvellous sense of physical movement compensated for the effort involved. Carrying only a daypack, Carol found the going much easier. The top of the headland was made up of a series of grassy slopes falling gently towards the precipitous cliffs. Small clumps of bushes were buffeted erratically by the wind. At the base of the cliffs, waves crashed upon the rocks unceasingly, the swirls of foaming water mesmerising me.

After walking for some time, it was a relief to sit down out of the wind and remove our packs. A spot of lunch was welcomed. We consumed our sandwiches, fruit and drinks. We lay on the soft grass, enjoying the warmth of the sun, the smell of the sea and the occasional calls of sea birds.

The path, which had followed the cliff-tops, turned inland near a quarry and merged with a narrow road through the tiny hamlet of Sandwith. Fortunately, the guidebook provided clear directions, as a number of alternative roads soon presented themselves. The path then followed an old railway line, now resurfaced with asphalt, allowing easy access for both walkers and cyclists. This led to Moor Row, an extended row of houses along a main street. We exchanged excited glances, the "Coast to Coast" signs confirmed that we were on course. We were definitely on our way!

In the distance stood tomorrow's challenge -the hill named Dent. From this distance Dent looked like the tonsured head of a monk or a balding man, its foothills covered by a green canopy of trees, leaving the summit bare to the sun and sky. In the foreground lay a long row of grey and white buildings, which provided a contrast with the greenery elsewhere. From behind a low escarpment, we heard the unmistakable sound of a cricket bat striking a hard leather ball, followed by shouts of fans urging their teams to victory. We were nearing the village of Cleator and its cricket ground. Further along the stony track, a stand of trees partially hid the lovely church of St Leonard.

No matter whether you're a novice or an experienced walker, it's always a relief to reach your first evening's stop. The excitement and physical activity of walking unaccustomed distances soon prepares the traveller for a well earned reward. Even though we had only walked nine miles, we were ready to stop.

Right now we wanted to find our B&B. But what a disappointment. Instead of scads of tea and hot scones, we found a typical bachelor's bungalow - which we declined. What to do? There were no other B&Bs in Cleator, so we phoned ahead to our next night's lodgings at Ennerdale Bridge. Yes, they could accommodate us and would even drive us back to Cleator the next morning.

The B&B at Ennerdale Bridge was a comfortable two-storey cottage owned by Geoff and Carole, a couple who had walked the coast to coast path. A refreshing pot of Geoff's special blend of walker's tea soothed the strains of the day away.

AD 436
Adventus Saxonum
< The Coming of the Saxons >

In 410 AD the Romans were forced to withdraw their troops from Britannia in order to defend their domains closer to Rome. The empire was being harried on all sides by a growing combination of forceful foes. The Huns, Goths, Vandals and Gauls were all pushing against the empire's boundaries with an insistent ferocity that could not be ignored. As the Romans withdrew from the island province, its inhabitants were left to fend for themselves.

The legions had gone forever. The superbly engineered roads they had marched across were neglected. With the Roman forts deserted, stonework from the now derelict buildings was used to construct fences and other fortifications.

The power vacuum in Britain attracted greater numbers of Teutonic peoples, known as Angles, Frisians, Jutes and Saxons (called the knifemen because of their sachs or long knives). These peoples who had tired of the harshness of their own terrains, were attracted by reports of richer lands where cultivation was easier, and began migrating.

Leaving their lands in Jutland (Denmark), Angeln (Belgium) and Frisia (the coastal part of Germany), they followed their own coastlines to where the sea crossing would be narrower. Here they crossed the channel and entered the navigable rivers and estuaries that indented the island's southeastern seaboard.

Once they had landed, the newcomers probably followed the Roman roads into the interior of the unfamiliar forest-covered land. Britain was a relatively fertile island that suited these invaders. Being suspicious of the former Roman structures, they made their own homes and paths, leaving the elements to claim the stonework left by the Romans. They cleared spaces within the forests, which were known as *leahs* or *leys*. Later communities established settlements higher up the valleys and these villages were called *tuns*. A *ham* was flat land close to a river.

The invaders settled and began to farm the land much like they had in their original homelands. New words replaced many of the earlier Celtic ones. Saxon suffixes included *worth* - enclosure, *den* - pasture, *hurst* - wooded hill, *burn* - stream, *ing* - settlement of people. For example, Kensington near London was named after the Saxons of Cynnesige.

They also brought a pantheon of Teutonic and northern gods representing the forces of nature and mankind's dreams and struggles. Odin the Allfather, also known as Woden, represented the sky. Frigg, his wife, was the earth goddess. Thor, also known as Thunor, was the god of the thunderstorm and Loki was the personification of fire. These gods quickly displaced the fledgling Christian religion, which had so far only developed a tenuous foothold in the lands formerly occupied by the Romans.

The invaders encountered little resistance. Only isolated and hardy groups of Britons attempted to repel them. This was the time of King Arthur. Many stories grew from the struggles between the Romano-Britons and the Anglo-Saxon invaders, which were later immortalised in the legends of Arthur and his knights. Terror and violence ensued. The Britons were driven westwards to the more isolated peninsulas and highland regions.

The invaders set about occupying some of the old Romano-British settlements such as Eboracum, and took control over most of the fertile areas of the island. Roman heritage and traditions were brutally swept away. The land was populated predominantly by heathens again. Odin and Thor triumphed over Christ. New languages and beliefs supplanted the older Celtic and Roman cultures and the days of the week were renamed after the invaders' gods.

Tuesday was named after Tew, the god of war, Wednesday after Woden

(Odin), Thursday after Thor and Friday after Frey, the god of rain and sunshine. Previously, the days of the week had been named after the planets visible to the Romans, such as Lundi-Luna-Moon (Monday), Mardi after Mars (Tuesday), Mercredi - Mercury (Wednesday), Jeudi - Jupiter (Thursday) and Vendredi after Venus (Friday). Saturday remained named after Saturnalia and Sunday after the sun.

Christianity did not disappear. It continued alongside worship of the Teutonic gods. The Britons who had been pushed into remote areas appear to have practiced a very early form of Christianity, which may have been brought over by Joseph of Arimathea. The pre-Roman religions had not been totally obliterated either. For instance, the worship of Eostre, the goddess of the Dawn, was wide-

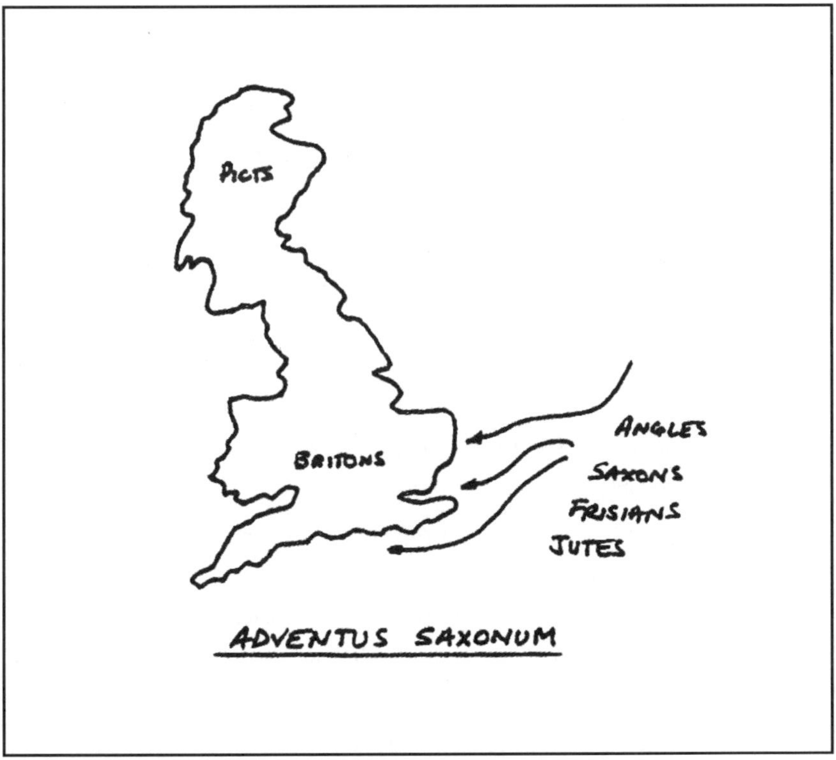

spread and her symbols, the hare and the egg represented spring and rebirth. Eostre was also known as Ostara by the invaders.

The invaders spread westwards and northwards, slaying and burning. More pirates from coastal Germany infiltrated the coasts and inland rivers exacerbating the atrocities. Vanquished native tribes were taken or sold into slavery resulting in a large slave class.

During the next 150 years, the Anglo-Saxons as they came to be called, established seven kingdoms - known as the heptarchy, consisting of Northumbria, Mercia, East Anglia, Kent, Sussex, Wessex and Essex. Of all the kingdoms, Wessex became the centre of power with its chieftain, Cerdic, establishing his dynasty there. Cerdic described himself as a descendant of Woden. It was characteristic of the Anglo-Saxon kings to trace their ancestry to divine origins. Cerdic claimed he was eight generations removed from Woden.

The Teutonic peoples believed that their gods were finite. They knew that the reign of their gods would end in a world-shattering event known as "The Doom of the Gods" when most of the old gods would be destroyed, leaving only the pure to survive and begin a new, more enlightened civilization.

⊕ To Ennerdale Bridge

Sunshine for the second day! Unbelievable. Geoff, our host at Ennerdale Bridge, drove us back to Cleator where we picked up the path from yesterday. But first a stop at the famous Cleator Pie Shop, the delicious odour of freshly baked pastry being irresistible.

Leaving Cleator, the road led through a sweet-smelling pine forest and then out onto the open slope of Dent, the hill we were to climb. Observing the exposed but luxuriant growth of these trees, I remembered reading that the pine tree was a symbol of immortality and strength of character because of its ability to withstand strong winds.

Surprisingly, Dent was an easy climb and we soon reached the top. The views across the Cumbrian plain to the distant, hazy Irish Sea were marvellous. Dent had two summits with a boggy area separating them. The guidebook requested walkers to take some stones from a nearby ruined wall and place them in the bog to reinforce a stone path that was being built to cross it.

As we made our way down the hill we were invigorated by the fresh smell of another pine forest. The track which zig-zagged through layers of fallen pine needles, was soft and moist underfoot, and the sun, filtering through the canopy above, illuminated tiny buzzing insects. At the bottom of the forest was a small stream with the lovely name of Nannycatch Beck. This stream wound its way through a narrow ravine passing beneath Ravencrag, an ominous, ragged outcrop of rocks. Eventually we walked out of the ravine onto a tarred road and saw an open field where the Kinnistone Stones stood, arranged in a circle. Unfortunately, this was not one of those pre-historic stone circles for which Britain and Ireland are well known. This circle had been placed by a 19th century archeologist to demonstrate a pet theory of his, and here they remained.

The persistent sun had left me with quite a deal of colour on my neck and arms. Carol wore a long-sleeved shirt and scarf, so had not been affected by the sun as much as I had. I had never associated England with sunburn. We walked along the road for a couple of miles until we reached Ennerdale Bridge. Tomorrow we would enter the Lake District - also known as Lakeland.

Geoff and Carole welcomed us for our second night with them. Over tea Geoff shared the secret of his recipe for this refreshing beverage; just mix a little Earl Grey with your regular blend, preferably the fine Yorkshire tea common in Northern England. As the tea was prepared and poured, it became clear that Geoff was a font of historical and local information. Over the evening we uncovered many things. The local language was explained - and I found that a *fell* was a hill and that the streams and smaller rivers were called *becks.*

"We expected the walk would be wet and difficult, but we've had excellent weather. Is this be normal?" Carol asked.

"May is often clear like this, and from my experience, you could have good weather for the next two weeks," he answered.

This was reassuring, as we had heard on the radio that rain and storms were wreaking havoc in Southern England.

In the lounge room there was more than enough reading material to keep us occupied - local walkers' magazines, books on various long distance walks and a selection of paperback novels. Perusing the bookshelf, I spied the biography of Alfred Wainwright - the man who had had the vision to combine many existing walks to create a complete coast to coast traverse of England.

In the introduction to his 'A Coast to Coast Walk' Wainwright wrote:

> *"The walk is one I have long had in mind and in 1972 finally accomplished."*

He explained that he had written the guide to:

> *"Devise a pleasant enough route for the longer distance walker to traverse this latitude of England and see the marvellous sights whilst enjoying the physical activity entailed in doing so."*

Wainwright had spent most of his life walking and exploring the wilderness areas of Britain and was a prolific writer and a meticulous illustrator, even producing his own maps. His vision had motivated countless walkers to follow his coast to coast path and inspired others to devise their own routes.

AD 440
Saxon Life

The Anglo-Saxon invaders settled the new lands, maintaining their traditional Teutonic hierarchies. Each community consisted of a warrior-king who would reward his followers by sharing the newly acquired land and any loot that they were able to plunder. The thanes (thegns) were next in line and formed a group called the Witan whose purpose was to advise the warrior-king. Slightly below the thanes were the churls, the artisans or land-owning farmers who in times of trouble could be called upon to fight in the Fyrd - the Anglo-Saxon army. Next were the landless peasants (serfs) who worked for the thanes and received a share of the harvest. At the bottom of the ladder were the thralls (slaves), who were either captured enemies, criminals, or children sold into slavery. The thralls had no rights, no land, nothing. Perhaps the word "enthrall" springs from this.

Life was difficult for everyone. For workers in the fields, the hard manual labour was relieved by a short rest, and a slice of bread accompanied by a few bites of an onion or a garlic bulb. This meagre meal would evolve into what we know as the "Ploughman's Lunch." As well as being an important food, the onion was also seen as a symbol of revelation; as in peeling away its layers to reveal its centre. Its strong smell was used to ward off evil.

The newcomers also brought their own ideas of law and order. A suspected wrong doer would have to attend a moot (meeting) in which the villagers would formally accuse the suspect. If the crime were admitted, punishment was meted out. If denied, the accused would have to prove innocence.

This was a risky move. The accused was given two alternatives, trial by iron or by water. The ordeal by iron involved the defendant carrying hot irons, or walking on red-hot plough shares. The defendant's limbs were then bandaged. If the wounds healed without festering, innocence was declared. If on the other hand, there appeared any unhealed burning or blemishes from the hot irons, the accused would be punished.

Ordeal by water began with the defendant drinking sacred water and then being thrown into the river. Drowning proved innocence. Trial by hot water involved the accused thrusting his arm into boiling water to snatch a stone, and if it was withdrawn without hurt, the accused was declared not guilty.

Around 588, having pushed the Britons to the extremities of the island, the Anglo-Saxons turned to warring amongst themselves. Aethelbert, King of the Jutes established himself in Kent and declared his overlordship. His Frankish wife Bertha was a Christian who helped provide an opening for the re-establishment of Christianity on the island.

Abbot Augustine arrived in 597 to preach Christ's word. A year later Aethelbert was baptised and Christianity began to re-make its slow way through the island. Both pagan and Christian Anglo-Saxons were superstitious. Magic was a part of their everyday life. People felt relatively safe in the villages and towns but in the forests and uninhabited places, demons and monsters lurked. Common folk travelled only when absolutely necessary although the military classes, carrying out their duties, travelled more frequently. Gods, demons and monsters moved across the land. The Anglo-Saxons believed that Woden stalked the hills and lowlands in his cloak and hood. He was the gallows god and would sometimes stop to view a body dangling from the gibbet at a crossroads. On dark and stormy nights he was often seen riding across the skies leading a pack of lost and troubled souls.

Around this time Beowulf, an Anglo-Saxon poem, was written, which told of a young warrior's struggle with a monster. The poem tells of a monster named Grendel, who was creating a lot of trouble for a Danish king. Every night the monster would break into the king's sleeping hall and kidnap a number of the king's retainers. This had been going on for some time.

A young warrior named Beowulf heard of this and decided he would make his mark by dealing with the monster. Beowulf sailed from Sweden to Denmark and presented himself to the King. The king was relieved that somebody had arrived to help rid him of the monster.

The next night the young warrior waited in the darkness of the sleeping hall for the monster's return. Soon enough he heard the ripping of wooden beams as a large hairy arm split open the door and in came Grendel.

Beowulf experienced a shiver of awe and fear at the sight. He raised his sword and let out a war scream. Grendel turned around and saw him. He moved towards his opponent and quickly swiped the sword from Beowulf's grasp. As the combatants struggled across the hall, Grendel realised that he had found his match. The monster's one weakness was that he had to return to his cave on the moors before dawn, or he would die in the presence of the rising sun.

Grendel knew that time was running out. He struggled towards the splintered door, but Beowulf held firm.

There was not much time left as the false dawn had begun. Grendel panicked, wrenching his massive arm from Beowulf with such force that it was torn from its socket as he escaped through the broken door.

The doomed Grendel staggered off to the moors, leaving a bloody trail.

* * *

The seven kingdoms had by now consolidated into the three larger ones of Wessex, Mercia and Northumbria. These now continued struggling for sole control of the island.

Around 756 the tenuous alliances between the kings of Mercia and Northumbria broke down and the northern region was torn asunder in a prolonged spate of lawlessness and bloodshed. Kings were betrayed and deposed by ambitious nobles who usurped their positions by force.

While the nobles were fighting for power, the common folk suffered in the wake of all the bloodshed and chaos. The land was neglected and fell to waste. It was as if all the useful energy of the land had been absorbed into the maelstrom of the battle for power.

With the land laid waste, famine was followed by plague. The troubled north was now alienated from the more settled south.

⊕ To Lakeland

Our second morning with Geoff and Carole at Ennerdale Bridge dawned bright and clear. As we lingered over breakfast our hosts told us of their many walking holidays both at home and abroad. Prior to running the B&B, they had owned a petrol station, but demand had dropped off, so they took up servicing the needs of walkers passing through this area. As we farewelled our hosts, Geoff re-iterated that the weather should hold steady for a week or even longer.

Lakeland lay just ahead of us. It had held a mystical fascination for poets and writers throughout the centuries and I was keen to see what all the fuss was about. Wordsworth, Blake and Coleridge, to name a few, had all lived in or visited the area, and each in turn had written endearingly of its character and manifold charms.

An asphalt road led to a dirt track that turned off in front of a small farm. The owner, taking a break from his work, asked us where were we from. We told him we were Australians.

"Oh, from Australia. I've got a niece there, but I've never had the time to visit her," he said, echoing a similar refrain expressed by other Cumbrians we had met over the past few days.

Next to the farm was a sturdy wooden bridge with which to cross a clear stream. Further along the track we greeted a couple of British walkers and their Border Collie dog enjoying a rest in the brilliant sunshine. We continued until we reached the edge of Ennerdale Water, the first of the lakes. The water looked dark blue and refreshing, but too cold for a swim. On the other side of the lake, the sun shone down on the bare green fells. The track followed the southern edge of the water, ascending and descending over the rocky contours. Primroses grew in a sheltered niche between two large rocks. The primrose was the prima rosa - the first rose, which heralded Spring. In Teutonic folklore it was believed that one who wore a primrose would find a hidden treasure.

Before long we had left the elongated strip of Ennerdale Water behind and walked into the pine plantation known as Ennerdale Forest. Using the guidebook and checking the signs, we followed a forestry road, which started to climb uphill, slightly diverging from the gurgling River Liza below. The wide dusty road was fringed with tall pines and the boisterous chirping of birds added a tingling resonance to the air.

There were two well-known options for this section of the walk. The first one was the more challenging, in which heroes could ascend to the high route and trek along the ridge tops taking in the peaks of Red Pike, High Stile, High Crag and Hay Stacks - these being considered only a moderate challenge for experienced fell walkers. The other option was to follow the River Liza Trail for a longer distance and then perspire one's way up the fells to meet the first trail near Blackbeck Tarn.

Geoff and Carole had shown us a third option which involved a less arduous climb, but also included the peak called Hay Stacks. When they had proposed including Hay Stacks in the route I had no idea why, but I would find out later. Anyway, their suggested route suited us so we set out to follow it. After walking a mile or so, the river seemed to be further away from our track than when we had started, so we stopped to check the map. I reckoned that we had taken a higher road than the one suggested, so we improvised a path down through the cleared hillside towards the river, where we welcomed the shade of the trees. In the middle of the river was a cool spot on a large rock reached by a convenient set of stepping stones where we sat down and listened to the gentle gurgling of the water as it flowed around the rock.

Watered and refreshed we followed the well defined track along the riverbank. Soon enough a path appeared on the left, which would take us up to Scarth Gap and thence to Hay Stacks. Walking through a cooling stand of pine trees, we emerged onto a steep rocky incline, which continued all the way to Scarth Gap. During frequent rests along the ascent we turned around to enjoy the spectacular views of Ennerdale Water. Enclosed by two high ridges, the fell sides were partially clothed in pines. Above the tree line rocky protrusions were exposed to the elements. Upwards we climbed, towards the outcrops known as Hay Stacks. This difficult part of the track had been well maintained. In some places steps had been chipped into the rock, or extra stones placed as needed. We drew abreast of an overweight young man carrying a large backpack. His face was red from exertion and he looked as if he was about to have a heart attack. Carol expressed concern.

"I'm O.K. I'm just a slow walker," he replied. He told us he was on a short holiday from his job in Manchester.

"You'd better pass me," he advised. "I'm taking it easy up this slope."

From this vantage point, the delicate water of Buttermere was visible to the north. A little further along the track we saw a tarn - a small mountain pool - alongside which other walkers were resting and enjoying nature's visual feast. And so would we. We were on a bare ridge of upthrusted rocks. On the other side of the valley, weathered remnants of ancient mountains stood silently. The whole valley looked as if a glacier had scooped it out during the last ice age.

I had to get a photo. Right on cue Kelland, a young American photographer doing a stint for the Royal Geographic Magazine, appeared. We exchanged cameras, each photographing the other with the splendid view in the background.

We continued on the well-defined path along the royal ridges. This was absolutely marvellous walking. Up here under the sun, with just enough wind to remove any perspiration, the scenery was still unbelievable. I felt as if I was close to the top of the world. On the left were the steep slopes of Green Crag. We had to be careful with our footing. One false step would mean disaster - with only a mass of sharp, unforgiving rocks to arrest our fall. A little further on we came to a large tarn, guarded by a friendly goose that followed us in the hope of a feed. Maps don't always make sense. If this was Blackbeck Tarn, it should have been on our

Ennerdale Water lay in front of us.

left. Maybe we had misread the map, but we were still in the right area. However, the map clearly showed the position of Hay Stacks. Looking back at the great roll and jumble of rocks we had just left, they looked just like a number of untidy haystacks.

Carol then told me the significance of Hay Stacks. She said it was one of Wainwright's favourite places. In his will he had requested that his ashes be sprinkled over those rocks and when he died a few years ago, his family carried out his wishes.

The area was also well known for its abundance of Honister slate, which had been extracted from these high areas for many years. We walked through an old slate quarry and climbed up a steep track hewn from a heap of discarded slate

pieces. These pieces of slate would probably be worth a small fortune back in town.

Over the past few hours we had taken numerous rest stops and had expected the overweight walker to have caught up with us, but he was no-where to be seen. We hoped that he had not suffered any mishap. The fells have claimed walkers over the years.

Our route followed a disused tramway up a steady gradient, which led to another ridge pass. The sun had passed its zenith and was beginning to cast longer shadows. We were tired but relieved to know that the remainder of the day's walk was downhill.

There was a steep descent to Honister Hause, the location of a working

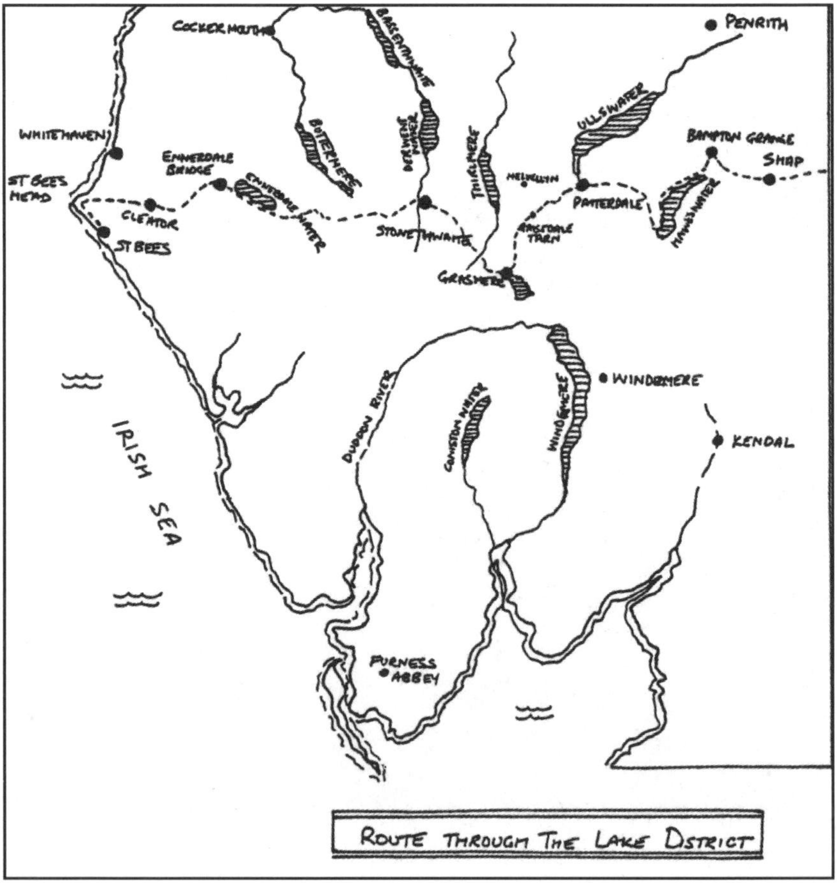

slate factory. Heavy slabs of slate were neatly stacked in the yard across from the office. Just below the tidy factory was the Honister Youth Hostel, where we obtained some urgently needed water and sat down for a brief rest. I had my boots off airing my feet when I recognized the familiar form of the Mancunian as he walked through the door. I asked him how he was and he replied, "tired, but satisfied at having walked the distance to Honister."

Good. We wouldn't be reading about the fells claiming another walker.

The next village down the track was Seatoller; a charming potpourri of buildings, one of them clearly inscribed with the date 1612. We were too tired to fully appreciate Seatoller as we still had another mile or two of walking before reaching our next night's lodging at Stonethwaite. By this stage of the day I just wanted to reach our destination, shed my pack and relax. My level of appreciation had diminished rapidly and I stopped just short of accepting a lift, if there was one to be had!

Luckily, the map showed a shortcut to Stonethwaite, which we took. In the late afternoon, Stonethwaite looked like a village that had miraculously sprung up from the rocky land surrounding it. Only some farm machinery indicated that the twentieth century had made inroads here. The cottages and ivy-covered barns cast a spell on us. Ahead was "Knotts View Cottage". As soon as we arrived on the doorstep, Carol eagerly pressed the doorbell. Anne, our hostess, opened the cottage door revealing a magic interior. Thick walls, uneven floors, low beamed ceilings, busily patterned carpets and quaint lights – it was like a gingerbread house from a fairy tale. All that was missing were the elves.

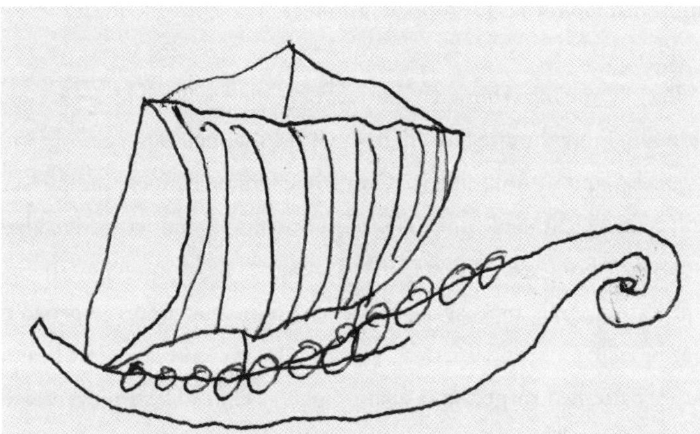

Time on the Tree of Life

GYFU
(the gift)

As the terrible days and nights passed, Odin swayed at the end of the cord and his mind filled with constantly changing thoughts and memories.

Being the god of the underworld and ruler of the dead and unborn, he remembered how he would sometimes travel in disguise to visit his domains. During these times, travellers could encounter him as a tall figure, wrapped in a cloak with a drawn hood. Odin thought about his power to raise the dead and his ability to change shape, often travelling in the form of a wolf or a raven.

Odin thought of the giants. They were created along with the gods but had always been adversaries. The giants lived on the perimeter of the world and grasped at any chance to better the gods. The frost giants were the worst. They tried all sorts of tricks to gain entrance to Asgard and partake of the lifestyle they believed was their birthright. They caused the great ice sheets to settle over the earth during the dark winter months.

Then there were the dwarves. They had all been created from a dead giant's flesh. The dark and cunning ones were banished to the dark recesses of the earth where they spent their time fossicking and collecting all types of precious subterranean metals and gems. The lighter dwarves called elves and fairies were generally benevolent little folk, and lived in a transparent place between Asgard and earth.

Odin thought of the exasperating Loki, an offspring of the frost giants who was sometimes mistaken for a god because of his powers to change shape at will. Loki was sometimes so attractive and ingratiating that Odin had made him a blood brother to the gods, but had since regretted his impulsive generosity. Loki was also the king of troublemakers. Gods and men did not trust him because of his constant trickery and treachery. He was inevitably involved in most of the problems encountered by the gods.

Loki had secretly married a giantess named Anguish, who bore him three amazing and frightening offspring - an eerie daughter named Hel, an unusual serpent and a wolf called Fenris. He kept these children a secret from the gods as long as he could, but they grew so fast that they soon could no longer be confined to their dark cave. Odin became aware of their existence and decided to rid the world of them in case they became a threat to Asgard.

He banished Hel into the depths of Niflheim, a dreary ice-cold place, and allowed her to reign over the nine dismal worlds of the dead.

He threw the serpent into the sea where, to Odin's amazement, it flourished and grew so large that it encircled the world, finally grasping its own tail in its mouth. It held the world together and if it ever became dislodged, unimaginable troubles would result. The serpent lay wrapped around the world, but had not forgotten Odin's unfriendly treatment.

He brought Fenris the wolf to Asgard where he planned to domesticate him. The gods were none too pleased when they saw the ferocious wolf, except Tew, the god of war who was unafraid. As Fenris grew in size and ferocity, any idea of taming him quickly evaporated. Odin remembered how the gods decided they would capture and get rid of Fenris.

They obtained a strong chain and playfully proposed to Fenris that they would test his strength by seeing if he could break it. Fenris knew that the chain would present no obstacle and allowed himself to be bound. When all were ready, Fenris snapped the chain with a mighty stretch. The gods were not pleased, but they concealed their worries by complimenting the wolf on his strength. A stronger chain was produced and again, although this time reluctantly, Fenris agreed to be bound. The wolf found it a little more difficult, but with another mighty stretch managed to break the chain.

The gods were now alarmed. Realising that a special bond would need to be made for Fenris, they sought out the dark dwarves and asked them to fashion a fetter for the wolf. Being skilled at such things, the dwarves created a thin flexible strand from rare essences - a cat's footsteps, the roots of a mountain and the voice of fishes. This was a special bond because the more it stretched the stronger it became.

The gods took the slender strand from the dwarves and again proposed to test the wolf's ever growing strength. Along with his increased size and ferocity, Fenris had also become more wily. He agreed to the test, on condition that one of the gods would put his hand between his fangs as a guarantee that there was no trickery on their part.

Since none of the gods would take the challenge, Tew stepped forward and plunged his arm between Fenris' dangerous jaws. The slender strand was then used to bind Fenris. The wolf tried to break the bond but found that he had been tricked. So he bit Tew's hand off.

The gods dragged Fenris off and chained him to a rock in a deep chasm. To silence his terrible howls, Frey jammed his sword in between the wolf's open jaws. Fenris was destined to remain chained like this until the final day. Meanwhile, the one-handed Tew went off to plan further battles as if nothing had happened.

The gods had unwittingly created two vengeful enemies - the serpent and Fenris - an action, which would have disastrous consequences in the future.

On the ninth night, when his time on the tree was almost complete, Odin looked down to the base of the tree. In amongst the roots he saw some glowing stones. He summoned what was left of his strength and stretched down into the mysterious spaces between the roots, bending the branch he was hanging on. The stones were almost within his reach, so with a final mighty effort he grasped them. Having stretched out further than was possible, he screamed in agony as he finally dislodged them from amongst the tree roots. The knot holding the cord tied to the trunk, loosened and slipped, and Odin fell back onto the icy ground gasping and heaving. His ravens left their perch, flew down and pecked at the stones to test their edibility. Finding them inedible, the ravens hopped over to Odin and welcomed him back after his ordeal by cawing loudly. These glowing stones, on which he could see the magical runes inscribed, were what he had been seeking. He now had the secret alphabet.

⊕ To Grasmere

In the delightful dining room of the Stonethwaite cottage, Ann shared some of her family's history with us over a hearty breakfast. Four hundred years ago the church owned vast tracts of land which needed to be cultivated. The monks from Furness, an area in southern Cumbria, built this row of cottages to house the workers and their families. Eventually this cottage came into the hands of her in-laws' predecessors and was now owned by the National Trust, with her family having guaranteed tenancy. Her husband's grandfather used to work in the quarries at Honister. He would walk up there in the morning, put in an eight hour shift and return that evening, six days a week year in year out. Life was tough in those days.

With the taste of a delicious marmalade still lingering, we set off towards the well-known Lakeland town of Grasmere. We crossed Stonethwaite Bridge to the north bank of Greenup Gill, followed by a steady climb along a thin gravel path up the valley. Above us, fleecy clouds had deflected the sun's direct rays and a cool wind removed all perspiration. A brief stop at Lining Crag refreshed us enough for the final ascent to Greenup Edge, the highest point of today's walk.

Austere views: fells and peaks with a total absence of any vegetation. Valleys, rivulets and exposed rocks. We gazed upon a fractured and worn landscape whose charm was inescapable. I could make out the tiny shapes of walkers ahead of us on the distant ridges. Clouds brushed the tops of the jumbled peaks and I sensed the moistness they left in their wake. It was almost unbelievable. I had to touch the ground with my hands to make sure that I was not in a dream or watching a wilderness documentary on television.

Up at these heights there were other walkers and we again met the British couple, Zillah, her son Tim and Doris their Border Collie, who kept darting around and sniffing at everything in sight.

"What an interesting walk so far," Zillah greeted us.

"It's magnificent," agreed Carol. "Where are you heading to?"

"To Grasmere today and Patterdale tomorrow," said Zillah. Tim and Zillah were making their way to Keld, which was the halfway mark of the Coast to Coast Walk. On previous holidays they had walked the Keld to Robin Hood's Bay section. We were pleased to discover that they would be staying at the same farm as ourselves in Patterdale the following night. The four of us agreed to meet there for dinner. Doris wagged her tail as if she knew of the feast ahead.

After this pleasant interlude at Greenup Edge, there was further to go. The ridge walk continued alongside Calf Crag, Gibson Knott and Helm Crag. From here another surreal view presented itself. Down below were the narrow roads and green fields with the town of Grasmere extending along the banks of its namesake - the lake of Grasmere. Through the crystal clear air, the little town seemed so close that you could almost reach out and touch it. A couple of airforce jets screamed overhead, causing us to cover our ears from the blast. Seeing the armed forces patrolling British skies against possible, if improbable foreign attack promoted a sense of security and reminded me of earlier Anglo-Saxon invasions.

It took some time to pick our way carefully down the steep, winding path from Helm Crag until we arrived at a flat, sealed roadway that led to the heart of Grasmere, home for many years to William Wordsworth, one of England's best known poets.

It was a pretty town, which, although it catered for tourists, did not seem unduly spoiled by its popularity. In earlier times, pigs were herded near the lake and the name Grise Mere came about, "grise" meaning pigs. And so the name Grasmere evolved.

The temperature had dropped markedly since our descent from Helm

Crag and, stopping briefly to look at a shop window, we both realised how cold and tired we were. By now it was four o'clock. We were keen to visit Wordsworth's cottage and museum and today was our only chance. The Tourist Bureau supplied a map of the town showing the location of the cottage and we hurried there. We made it just in time to join the last tour for the day.

It was impossible not to be caught up in the enthusiasm of our young volunteer guide.

Wordsworth, one of five children, was born in the Lake District and was to leave an indelible mark on English poetry. Wordsworth enjoyed exploring the fells and rivers of his native land but yearned to visit Europe.

In 1790, when he was twenty, he embarked on a walking tour of Europe with a friend. This was the era of the Grand Tour, when young men of society travelled to view the great sites of the continent.

William and his friend started their walk in Lyons, France. They climbed

Near Hay Stacks - the delicate water of Buttermere

Mont Blanc, continued on to the Alps and across to Lake Como. Wordsworth was a tireless walker, often covering forty miles in a day. They made their way back to Switzerland and steered a boat down the Rhine to Cologne and walked through Belgium to Calais. After this they returned to college life at Cambridge. For the next decade, Wordsworth would walk many miles in appreciation of nature and his search for man's relationship with it.

On another walking tour, William, accompanied by his sister Dorothy and the poet Coleridge, travelled to Germany, where William and Dorothy undertook a long journey through the Harz Mountains.

In 1799 Wordsworth again accompanied by Coleridge, came upon an old disused inn "The Dove and Olive Branch", in Grasmere. The timing was impeccable. Wordsworth was able to use the income from an inheritance to rent the inn, which became his home for many years enabling him to continue his literary career. The name of the inn was a biblical reference to the dove, which returned to Noah's ark carrying an olive branch after the flood. The name was shortened to "Dove Cottage" and William and Dorothy settled there. Life at the cottage became quite full, with William's marriage to his childhood sweetheart, Mary, children and countless visitors. The entourage eventually had to move to larger quarters.

After an enthralling tour of Dove Cottage, it was time to find our own refuge for the evening, a delightful B&B just out of town.

* * *

The next morning, as I lay in a drowsy state, the words of a popular Wordsworth poem floated into my mind.

I wandered lonely as a cloud
That floats on high o'er Vales and Hills,
When all at once I saw a crowd
A host of dancing Daffodils;
Along the lake, beneath the trees,
Ten thousand dancing in the breeze.

From the elegant breakfast room, Wordsworth's lonely cloud was n'er to be seen that morning. Our fellow breakfasters were an American couple who had walked the Coast to Coast path three years ago. Every year they return to Grasmere for a couple of weeks to indulge their passion for daily rambles in the district.

Bob, our host, brought us food and regaled us with stories of his maritime days travelling the world as a "chippie" and later as a fiddler with a musical group. I asked Bob whether B&B owners ever ate their own fare.

"No way," he replied. "If I did, I'd be the size of a horse."

Since the unexpectedly good weather had caught us unprepared, it was necessary to buy some sunscreen lotion as both of us were beginning to look as red as English postal boxes.

We consulted our map for today's route. First we were to climb to Grisedale Tarn and from there we had three options. The brave at heart could climb one of Lakeland's best known peaks, Helvellyn. The second option was to stride out along the neighbouring mountain route of St Sunday Crag, and the last option and least arduous - which we chose - was to follow the Grisedale Valley into Patterdale.

Occasionally Carol and I liked to walk separately, to experience some time alone. In this mode I began the ascent to Grisdale Tarn. The sun was warm and a slight wind kept the air fresh. My boots felt comfortable and my fitness much improved from the first day at St Bees.

Near a waterfall the track divided, so I kept to the high side and walked past a crag named Hause Riggs. Up ahead I could see a gap in the fells indicating a pass. This would be a good place for a breather. Over the ridge of the gap I met two other walkers having a rest. We chatted about the walk and one of them, a Scot, asked, "When you were up at Haystacks, did you get any dust in your eyes?" I was puzzled.

"It may have been a piece of Wainwright!" he chortled. I laughed, finally getting the joke.

A little further on was the dark water of Grisedale Tarn. Here I caught up with Carol and we ate our sandwiches in the embracing sunshine. On our left was the huge climb to Helvellyn and glory, while the remote peak of St Sunday Crag was visible on the right. Tiny figures resembling stick insects were slowly making their way along the distant ridges. For a moment an errant thought crossed my mind, maybe we should try the Helvellyn ascent. However, the relaxing sun and gentle breeze soon blew that thought away.

Near the track was a large rock known as the "Brothers Parting Stone". It was on this spot that William and Dorothy had farewelled their beloved brother, John. John was off to Penrith, en route to take command of a ship in the English fleet. He was never to return to Dove Cottage, as he drowned a few years later when his ship was wrecked. Inset was a weathered, unreadable plaque, but the spirit of departure remained. In Dorothy's journal dated September 29th 1801, she wrote:

"John left us. Wm. and I parted with him in sight of Ullswater. Poor fellow, my heart was right sad. I could not help thinking we should see him again, because he was only going to Penrith."

Up here were the flowers that John Wordsworth had loved, like the daisies which grew near the tarn. Daisies were originally known as "Day's Eyes" an emblem of Freya, the northern goddess of rain and sunshine, and they represented innocence.

As we descended along the green Grisedale Valley, we could see Patterdale in the distance. The valley had a delightfully pastoral feel to it with the sheep munching grass alongside their newly born lambs and the birds twittering in the clean, crisp air. The sheep were hardy Herwicks, bred from the original Viking flocks. The valley flattened out near Patterdale.

Patterdale had the quality of an alpine village. The imposing fells formed a backdrop to the steady pines. I felt as if we were in an English village that had been transplanted to Switzerland.

It was still early in the afternoon, so there was time to visit St Patrick's church, and we enjoyed the soothing classical music being played inside. Patterdale was once known as Patricksdale and tradition has it that St. Patrick, having been wrecked near the Duddon Sands on Cumbria's southern shores, made his way to this lovely spot. He stayed here long enough to baptize the locals, before continuing on his peripatetic way.

The mind creates expectations, and having reached town, I assumed that the night's accommodation was close by, so my muscles began to relax in anticipation, prematurely as it happened. Noran Bank Farm was another mile or so out of town. Along the road we crept, past the Patterdale Hotel, past the magnificent White Lion Inn, and even past the Youth Hostel. From this end of town, Patterdale resembled a compact medieval kingdom, complete with castle towers provided by the White Lion's chimneys. The imposing backdrop of the fells seemed to compress the kingdom even further.

Finally around another bend we saw our B&B, a whitewashed two storey farmhouse built up hard against the fells. A friendly dog wagged its tail and announced our arrival with a few mellow barks. The lady of the farm welcomed us and showed us to our room. A very welcome cup of tea brought on a speedy recovery, aided further by the arrival of Zillah and Tim, with a weary Doris at their heels.

During dinner at the Patterdale hotel, which allowed pets, we shared our day's experiences. Where we had followed the Grisedale Valley down to Patterdale, our companions had taken the hero's challenge and walked to the top of Helvellyn with Doris. That was something to celebrate. So tonight we would eat and drink the good produce of the land. Carol and Zillah ordered steak and ale pies with fresh garden vegetables, Tim a feast of Cumberland sausages and I chose a good old Ploughman's. Doris had already been fed, but her nose twitched in pleasurable anticipation every time a new meal was brought out from the kitchen.

I had eaten plenty of Ploughman's lunches before and always enjoyed them. My favourite was the cheese and pickle one, with fresh bread and lots of salad. A Ploughman's was never complete without at least three pints of cider or ale. Tonight was no exception.

"Well done," I congratulated our companions for climbing Helvellyn, "It must have been some climb."

"It wasn't too bad," Tim replied matter-of-factly, now feeling relaxed after his second pint.

"Doris did very well," Zillah added. "She literally ran up to the top." Doris lay contentedly at her mistress's feet, occasionally opening an eye at the mention of her name.

Feeling some regret that we hadn't taken the opportunity to tackle the most climbed mountain in England, I rationalised our decision by recounting Wainwright's words describing the ascent: "The gradient eases after an eternity of toil!."

In the same bar I saw the Scotsman and his walking companion, with whom we'd shared that joke about Wainwright near Grisdale Tarn. They were in fine spirits and seemed set for a long evening, propped up against the bar within earshot of the barmaid.

AD750
Food in Anglo-Saxon Times

The basis of power in all agricultural societies was rooted in the land and the Anglo-Saxons were no exception. The land supported the people; everything they needed came directly or indirectly from it - food, clothing, shelter. Surplus produce was sold or bartered for other goods and services.

A man who owned much land could rent it to others. Tenants were tied to the landowner by an arrangement of reciprocal protection in times of trouble.

The people mostly ate grains. The word "lord" derives from "keeper of the bread", while "lady" from "kneader of the bread". The poorer folk existed on barley and oats while the rich ate wheat. The Anglo-Saxons understood and used yeast for baking. Vegetables such as onions, garlic, turnips and cabbage were cultivated. Wild produce was seasonally available and a necessary supplement to the diet. Apples, berries and plums were favourites. The consumption of fish helped maintain the health of coastal communities and rivers provided freshwater fish and eels for inland folk.

"we gazed upon a fractured and and worn landscape..."

Meat was available to most communities. Pigs were popular as they could easily fend for themselves and pork lent itself to salting for extended storage over the winter months. Chickens, eggs and mutton also featured in the diet. Horsemeat was prohibited by the Christian Church because of its associations with old pagan feasts and sacrifices.

Salt, named after Salus, the Roman goddess of health, was the only easily available spice. The people obtained it from salt pans. Herbs were cultivated for many purposes. Monks labouring in the monasteries created many interesting and health promoting herb gardens. Sage, prized for its healing properties, Rosemary, Thyme, Mustard, Dill and Fennel. Because of its long germination time, Parsley's roots were thought to grow all the way down to the devil's lair. Imports from the East like Pepper, Cloves and Cinnamon were extremely expensive because of their rarity.

Sugar was unknown and the only readily available sweetener was honey. Beer was the most common beverage, followed by mead, which was made from honey and considered a favourite tipple of the northern gods. Tasty and aromatic ciders were also produced in some communities to the refrain of:

Old apple tree,
Old apple tree.
We come to wassail thee!

Many Anglo-Saxons remained pagans but there was a gradual conversion towards Christianity. Christian missionaries had established a number of monasteries during these years of interminable fighting and the region of Northumbria hosted two of the most famous of these at Lindisfarne and Jarrow, both on the East Coast. The Church had a settling effect on the brutish and largely coarse attitudes of the Anglo-Saxon tribes, and alongside the skirmishes, learning and literature were blossoming.

Out of this period came a profusion of Anglo-Saxon art especially from within the monasteries, where the crafting of golden chalices, silver plate vessels and all sorts of elaborately decorated metalwork was encouraged. Texts began to be written detailing the history of the land. They would later become a corpus of information known as the Anglo-Saxon Chronicle.

Even with the spread of Christian beliefs, worship of natural surroundings remained, and the worship of forests, rivers and mountains played a significant part in the daily lives of the Anglo-Saxons. Customs such as the "master and the shoe" were performed at weddings.

The bride's father would remove one of his daughter's shoes and hand it to the groom. The groom would then smack his bride's face with the shoe, demonstrating that he was now responsible for her. Centuries later, this custom would evolve into a pair of old shoes being tied to the wedding car after the reception, clattering down the street.

A proliferation of churches attracted growing congregations. Many churches were built on former sacred sites and frequently the old pagan ceremonies were combined with the newer Christian ones. To people living in crude huts and hovels with dirt floors and sparse comforts, these churches with their solid stone walls, brightly coloured interiors and evocatively carved figures must have seemed like magnificent proof of the power of the new God.

The devoutly Christian poem, The Dream of the Rood was penned during this period. It tells of the poet's dream:

> *While all men lay sleeping, the poet dreamed of a wonderful cross, the very cross on which Christ was crucified. The Cross was now adorned with marvellous jewels and expensive brocades. Yet the dreamer could still discern the marks of the Crucifixion and the bloodstains. Moved to sorrow at this sight, the poet listened in wonder as the Cross began to describe its experiences from the time it was felled in a forest until it was positioned on top of a hill. Christ hastened to mount His cross in order to redeem mankind.*
>
> *Many men came from near and afar to pierce the Lord with weapons until His blood flowed and drenched the Cross. The sky grew*

dark and the earth trembled. All creation wept lamenting Christ's death. A tomb was hewn out of rock and he was laid to rest. The Cross was cut down and dumped into a deep pit where it was found by the Lord's followers. They then raised it up and bedecked it with gold and silver.

Lost Gods of England, Brian Branston

Even though Northumbria struggled in the midst of much angst and turmoil caused by sporadic fighting, it was still one of the brightest places of culture in Europe at the time. Unfortunately, the monasteries at Lindisfarne and Jarrow stood directly in the path of the coming horrendous onslaught.

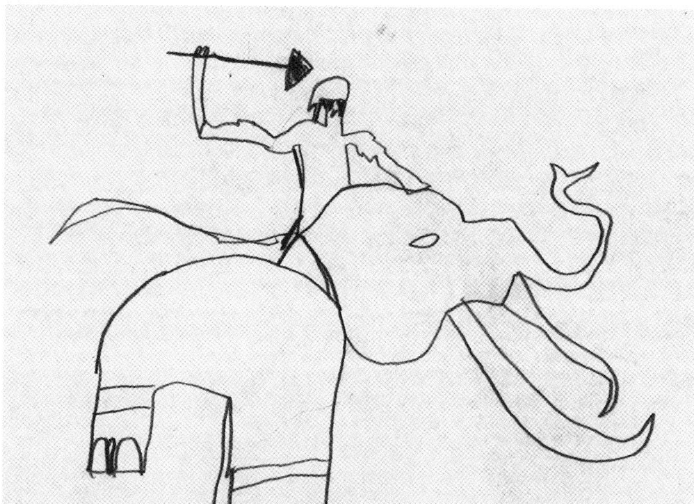

The Watchman of the Gods

ANSUR
(a prophecy)

After the ordeal of nine nights suspended from Yggdrasil, Odin finally had the runes. These were symbols that made up a magical alphabet that allowed the user to probe the future and to cast spells. Odin carved the shapes of the runes onto a wand and kept it near his chest. He would consult them by letting his fingers be drawn to the most appropriate rune to answer any question that arose.

He then taught the language of the runes to the other gods and in later times he passed on the alphabet to the seers and poets of the world.

For the time being, Odin was in need of a rest, so he visited the seashore for its restorative qualities. Walking along the beach, he spied nine beautiful maidens lying asleep on the white sands. The nine maidens so filled him with lust that he woke them up and announced that he would marry them all at once. The maidens giggled and eagerly agreed to Odin's proposal. In due course, between them they bore a son named Heimdall.

Because he was fed all the good things of nature, Heimdall quickly grew into a strong, honest and fearless god and soon joined Odin and the others in Asgard. It so happened that the gods had recently finished building Bifrost, the Rainbow Bridge that connected Asgard with earth and they were concerned that it was unguarded. Without a sentry on duty, the frost giants would be able to cross it and attack Asgard. Heimdall was only too pleased to take up the position of sentinel. His hearing was so acute that he could hear grass growing in the next valley and moreover, his sight was as good at night as it was during the day. He also needed very little sleep. To help him guard Bifrost, he was issued with a sword and a horn with which to alert the gods whenever any of their enemies approached.

The first opportunity to use his talents arrived one night when he was disturbed by a quiet footfall. He saw Loki standing by the bedside of the sleeping Freya. Around her neck was a shining string of pearls, which kept the earth fruitful. Loki was trying to unclasp the necklace, but the clasp was just out of reach under her neck. The skillful trickster changed into a flea and bit her, so that she turned without waking. He then gently unclasped the necklace and ran off with it.

Heimdall followed him, unsheathing his sword. He was about to cut off Loki's head, when the trickster changed into a flame, his real essence. Heimdall changed into a bowl of water to quench the flame, so Loki changed into a seal and dived into the sea. Heimdall followed him into the water and a struggle ensued. In the end Loki was forced to surrender the necklace, which was returned to Freya, ensuring that the earth would remain bountiful. Heimdall had made an enemy of Loki, but he also had Loki's measure.

Apart from his reknown as the watchman of Asgard, Heimdall had another talent. In some places he was known as Rig, "the father of humanity". As Rig, he helped in the creation of the three social classes:

Rig (Heimdall) enjoyed wandering about when he wasn't on duty at Asgard. One day he came upon a rundown shack and knocked on the wall, as there was no door. An elderly couple named Great Grandfather and Great Grandmother shuffled to the doorway to see who had come to visit them. They recognized Rig and invited him in. Although their clothes were old and worn and they had very little to share with Rig, he graciously accepted the broth and bread he was offered. After the meal, Rig stayed with the couple for three nights and shared their bed.

Nine months later, Great Grandmother gave birth to a son, who they named Thrall. Thrall grew up to be a swarthy, clumsy lad who later mated with a girl of similar proportions and temperament. They had a number of offspring who were nicknamed "Fatty", "Runny Nose" and "Pin Head." These became the slaves who performed all the hard and dirty tasks in the community. Often they were treated worse than the animals they cared for.

Rig's next stop was at a comfortable looking house where he met a cautious and industrious couple, Grandfather and Grandmother. After a hearty meal of bread, cheese and fruit, Rig shared their bed for three nights.

In due course, Grandmother gave birth to a strapping lad called "Karl" or Freeman. Karl in turn married a strong lass who wore a cape and kept a bunch of keys attached to her waist belt, which proved that she was a capable mistress of her household. Karl and his wife brought up a number of children with names like Smithy, Maiden, Strongman and Guard. These became the farmers who owned and managed the land.

Rig had one more visit to complete. He approached a large hall with a beautifully carved door set off by polished handles. He knocked on the door and was invited in by Father and Mother. He could see that the furnishings were of best quality and he sat down in the most comfortable of seats. Father was sturdy and handsome and Mother was elegant. Rig shared their meal of poultry and pork served with a lovely wine. As on the former occasions, Rig shared their bed for three nights.

In turn, nine months later, Mother gave birth to a son named Jarl. When Rig saw Jarl, he treated him like a son and taught him the Runes. Rig also taught Jarl to fight and acquire land. Jarl grew up to be a leader of men and married a lass who was his equal. Together they had twelve sons; the last one looked the image of Rig. They called him 'young Kon' or Kon nyg. His name evolved into "Koenig" or "King".

* * *

Odin was the god of wisdom. He had gradually acquired a measure of sagacity during his life by questioning all he met. Odin was always travelling, usually accompanied by his ravens. His continuing quest drew him to Mimir's spring, which was known to have magical properties. It conferred wisdom; understanding and the powers of prophecy upon all who drank of its waters.

The magical spring lay deep in a sheltered valley, and all who sought it seemed to be blind to its location. However, Odin found the spring, hidden by ferns and mosses. He made his way through the foliage and encountered the spring's guardian, Mimir.

Mimir challenged Odin, "Why do you seek these waters?"

"For the power of prophecy," replied Odin.

Mimir said, "You will have to exchange one of your precious possessions for a drink from this spring."

Odin was so intent on learning the secrets of prophecy that out of desperation, he swapped one of his eyes for a draught of the miraculous water. After drinking the water, he rested on the moss-covered rocks alongside the spring.

The magical waters began affecting him. He experienced a vision, in which Loki, the evil trickster accompanied by his horrible offspring Hel, goddess of the underworld, the Serpent and Fenris the wolf, together with a massive army of frost and mountain giants, finally confronted Odin and his fellow gods on the Plain of Vigrid.

A terrible battle ensued, in which the combatants destroyed each other, the earth was ravaged by fire and flood and all men perished. The reign of the gods had come to an abrupt end. This final battle was called Ragnarok, the "Doom of the gods".

Odin was perplexed and deeply concerned. If the prophecy of Ragnarok was correct, he had to find some way of averting or surviving it. He asked his two ravens for assistance and they suggested that he visit the Fates to seek their advice.

The three Fates, known as Urd (Past), Verdandi (Present) and Skuld (Future) dwelt by the sacred spring of Urd, located at the base of one of the roots of Yggdrasil, upon which Odin had hung for nine nights. Arriving at Urd, he asked the Fates whether Ragnarok was destined to occur.

The Fates replied, "Yes, indeed. Ragnarok was foretold."

"Is there nothing that can be done to avert doom?" Odin asked.

"We know of naught that will stop destiny," they replied.

The Fates added cryptically, "Everything changes."

Odin was numb. He asked, "What can I do?"

"Remember, the destiny of the gods is linked to your collective actions," they answered elusively.

"Will I survive?"

"Only through transformation," Skuld replied.

"How will I know when the end is nigh?" Odin persisted.

"You will know it when your son dies. Then the great snows will fall and disaster will visit the world," they said.

With the prophecy of his son's death ringing in his ears, the Fates dissipated in a thin smoky haze. For his troubles, Odin was left with an empty eye socket and a doomed future. He was able to cover the eye socket with strands of his steely grey hair. As for the future, he was at a loss to know what to do. And what did the fates mean by transformation?

AD780
The North People

The warriors from the north were known as "Vikings", "Norsemen" or "Norse". "Vik" in the Old Norse language means "one who frequents inlets of the sea". The Scandinavian landscapes of Norway and Sweden were bounded by the sea and indented by fjords and lakes. There was little flat land for farming; so much of their food had to be claimed from the sea. They bred hardy sheep for meat and wool, from which they spun thread for clothing.

The dark, scented pine forests plunged into the deep fjords. Waters from the melting snows flowed over high rocky ledges and cascaded into the icy cold waters of the North Sea. Up above this marvellous terrain of dark green and blue colours rose the mighty mountain ranges whose tops were covered by snow and ice. Such majestic and awesome sights had inspired the northerners to create legends and poems about their gods. The Norse viewed the universe as a place of constant tension between the forces of chaos and order. It was vitally important to them, to maintain the harmony between mankind and the constantly changing natural environment.

The landscape of Denmark (Jutland) was almost the reverse. Swamps and treacherous rivers covered it, and travel was mostly by boat. The winds that howled around the Jutish promontories had a particular energy about them, forcing the people to migrate.

Trouble had been brewing amongst the inhabitants of the far northern lands for some time. Their communities were experiencing rapid growth. The Northerners had opened eastern trade routes via the river systems of the continent as far as Kiev. To the west they used the Orkney and Shetland Islands as bases for further exploration and plundering. They brought back richly embroidered Mediterranean cloths, Germanic wines, Byzantine gold and silver ornaments, tangible benefits of trade and looting. They even traded human slaves.

Many aspects of their lives were recorded using the runic alphabet. The runes were part of their daily life. There were runes that invoked the gods' support for protection from enemies or for victory in battle. Other runes were used for material gain and to maintain good health. The people believed that Odin had found the runes amongst the roots of the Tree of Life and had passed them onto mankind.

The usage of runes became so integral to these communities, that the magicians and seers had a full time job in divining the future, healing, making and breaking spells and providing inspiration for their communities. The word "Rune" meant a whisper or a secret.

As the communities grew, the young men needed to be usefully occupied. Since the eldest son would inherit his family's land, the younger sons had to carve out their future elsewhere. Many of the young men joined Viking raiding bands - an outdoor university for the manly arts.

The Vikings from Denmark, Sweden and Norway were renowned for their brutal warfare. These races were invigorated by the cold northern climate, but they valued poetry as much as action. Their deeds and battles were described and glorified in their sagas.

In one saga it is told of a band of Vikings who after a horrific battle at sea with another Viking band are captured and prepare to face death at the hands of their captors. One after another they are beheaded.

> *Then suddenly, one warrior proclaims to the assembled captors, "watch my face as the axe bites into my skull and see that I will not blanch. You will see how brave I am." He didn't.*
>
> *Another Viking says that he will lift his right arm after his execution to show his strength. He didn't.*
>
> *One Viking with long fine blond hair asks for one of his captors to grasp hold of his fine hair and move it out of the way so that the axe will not spatter blood over it. As the axe comes down, the Viking wrenches his head so sharply that the axe swings down and cuts off the hands of the man who had grasped the hair. The captors are impressed by this show of courage and offer the fine haired Viking his freedom. He accepts it, but on condition that his remaining companions are also let free. The captors briefly discuss this unusual request and decide to release their prisoners.*
>
> Snorri Sturluson (Vikings! - Magnus Magnusson)

Stories were told of the brutal mutilations and savagery of the times. Conquered people and slaves would usually be quickly killed, but a special torture was kept for the kings and rulers of vanquished peoples. This was the legendary Blood Eagle where the captured ruler was forcefully laid upon a stone, ribs smashed apart, then his lungs would be cut open and spread out like an eagle's wings.

The Vikings, like their gods, were passionate and violent people who respected courage, strength and craftiness. There was even a warrior caste devoted to Odin, who called themselves "the berserkers" and wore wolf skins and animal pelts in battle. They would whip themselves into a frenzy before a battle and run screaming at their enemies twirling and thrusting their swords in all directions, tactics that made them seem invincible to their foes.

So, from the Norwegian fjords, Jutish estuaries and the wooden jetties of Sweden and the Baltic Isles, determined Viking fleets sallied forth in search of new adventures and plunder. The Swedes crossed the Baltic and explored the vast inland regions. The Norwegians sailed directly to the eastern coastline of Britain and also via the Shetland and Orkney Islands to Ireland. The Danes manoeuvered their sleek, black-hulled vessels down along the coasts of southern Britain and Gaul (France).

The Death of Balder

IS
(a freezing)

The most loved of all the gods was Balder, the god of light. He lived with his wife Blossom, the daughter of Bud, in a palace with a silver roof supported by golden columns. He had learnt the runes from Odin and had them engraved upon his tongue. Balder also possessed three magical accessories: the winged helmet of clear thought; a sword of clear intentions; and sandals of clear movement. He was a pleasure to be with, as in his presence gods and men found themselves imbued with clarity and a sense of purity rarely experienced.

One day his fellow gods noticed that his demeanor had changed. They grew uneasy, as this was the first time they had noticed melancholy in Balder. They asked him what the matter was.

"I have constant dreams in which I sense a great danger to my life," he said. "In my dreams, I see myself injured and dying. Then I see the world plunged into darkness."

The gods decided to find a remedy for his burden and went to tell the earth goddess Frigg, of her son's foreboding. After hearing of Balder's troubles Frigg set off to visit all worldly things and asked for their assurance that they would cause him no harm. She asked the earth, fire, the metals and wood, the trees and fish, all of the animals that roamed the fields and birds that flew in the sky. All the creatures and things of the world agreed that they would not harm Balder.

Frigg returned with the good news and the gods felt a sense of relief. When it was discovered that no materials could injure Balder, the gods found great enjoyment from hurling stones and weapons at him. The missiles would merely be deflected or miss him altogether. There was much laughter and gaiety in Asgard as Balder and his fellow gods would amuse themselves for many hours in this manner.

However, this merriment attracted Loki. He had heard the laughter and disguised himself as an old woman to investigate the source of the gaiety. The old woman approached Frigg who was busy spinning.

"What is the cause of all this mirth?" the old woman asked.

"The gods are enjoying testing Balder's newly found power," Frigg replied. "See, they can throw anything at him, yet he remains uninjured."

"How can this be?" the old woman asked, seeking to find an exploitable weakness in the situation.

"Because all things on earth have sworn not to injure Balder." The earth goddess replied.

"All things?" the old woman persevered. "Is there not one which has been missed?"

"Well, only the mistletoe, which is too young, and anyhow it grows quietly without harm," Frigg replied.

The old woman vanished. Loki had discovered the weakness in the gods' enjoyment. He found where the mistletoe was growing and broke off a stout little branch, which he fashioned into a strong, slender spike. Loki then approached the circle where the gods were enjoying themselves immensely by throwing missiles at Balder. He spied Balder's blind brother Hoder (the god of the dark), standing alone and quite dispirited.

"Why the glum face?" Loki asked.

"All the others are having fun throwing things at Balder." Hoder replied.

"Then why don't you join in?"

"I'm blind and anyhow, I have nothing to throw."

"Don't worry," said Loki. "I've got something for you. Just hold this little spear and I'll show you where to throw it." Loki turned Hoder in Balder's direction and guided his hand. Hoder threw the spike of mistletoe at Balder and it shot through the air.

The god of light groaned as the spike pierced his heart. Balder fell down dead. The mirth stopped. The gods were shocked; the fairest of them all had been struck down. Hoder was puzzled at the silence and did not understand when the gods seized him. Loki quickly disappeared.

⊕ Fell Walkers

The morning sun, creeping in through the lace curtains of our bedroom at Noran Bank Farm, assured us there would be no change in the superb weather. Downstairs, the breakfast room was an antique collector's delight. There were all sorts of knick-knacks decorating the walls and shelves. Our hostess, Sheila, had a vast collection of thimbles which friends and guests had added to over the years.

Studying our map over breakfast, we could see that it was going to be a long day - but not as long as Tim and Zillah's. Whereas they had already left to walk their 16 miles to Shap, we planned to walk the 12 miles to Bampton Grange. We had arranged to meet up with them again in the village of Osmotherly, a week's walk away.

We farewelled Sheila and retraced our steps past the village Post Office to the White Lion Inn from where the path continued.

What a pleasant day. Something about being here in the midst of this sunny valley filled me with unaccustomed joy. I felt good. My general well-being and increased physical stamina after five days of Lakeland walking had produced a feeling akin to euphoria in me. Carol also felt good.

The path crossed the stone bridge above Goldrill Beck and we slowly made our way up the fells towards Stony Rigg and Angletarn Pikes, the two peaks that overlooked the dark stain of Angle Tarn. The views were special. The solid eruptions of weathered fells beneath a stark blue sky lent a familiar sense of unreality to the region.

The previous evening, I had found a book on William. T. Palmer, an earlier fell walker who had lived in this district in the late 1800's. He had preceded Wainwright by a generation and was cast from the same mold. He loved to walk and read. And as he walked he made mental and written notes that he later used as the basis for many books and articles. Often ignoring marked routes he simply followed the contours of the land, travelling extensively across the British Isles.

He was of the firm opinion that, "the hills belong to all, and not just the few." When Palmer passed away in 1954, all was not lost, as the following year Wainwright's presence was announced with the publication of his "Pictorial Guide to the Lakeland Fells".

As we climbed higher, the imposing skyline of Satura Crag was visible on the left. A solid bank of clouds appeared like an army of grey soldiers and stationed themselves on the ridges. The small scoop of Hayeswater Lake glistened below. As

"Eruptions of weathered fells beneath a stark blue sky..."

we rounded a bend a large rocky outcrop known as The Knott, came into view. Meanwhile we became concerned about the ominous movement of the clouds. The grey mass seemed to be rolling in over the ridges above us. Since there was still some way to climb to the top, we hoped that the fog would not set in, as we knew of the difficulties other walkers had faced in similar circumstances. Our navigational equipment consisted of a compass, a strip map and the detailed guidebook. I hoped that we would not be put to the test.

As the wind rose the temperature dropped. We stopped and put on our wet weather gear and beanies. The wind relentlessly nipped at our ears. The gusting of the wind and the swirling of the clouds added to the beauty of this stark wilderness and I took photos to remind me that we had actually been here.

Continuing on around to the far side of The Knott we arrived at a saddle between two ridges. On the right was the magnificent fell, known as High Street. It was named after a Roman road, which followed the ridge. The Romans built their roads as straight as possible, following the most direct route over the fells, to avoid British ambushes.

As we stood on the saddle in the howling gale admiring High Street, Carol shouted: "What were the Romans doing up here when they could have been down in town enjoying lovely cream scones!"

"We should be down there too!" I yelled, shouting against the wind. A yellow tinge appeared, adding to the eeriness of the darkening sky. A corpulence of clouds hovering over the next set of ridges began to weep vertical plumes of rain over the fells.

Now came the final ascent to Kidsty Pike, at 2558 feet, the highest point of the day's journey. The clouds continued to roll in and the wind blew bitterly. We stopped again to add another layer of clothes as insulation against the cold. I could hear the roar of the wind in my hood as loose cords were sent into a frenzied flap. We reached the summit and appreciated the 360-degree views. The summit was the meeting point for a number of tracks. Just below and to the left I could see the path, which would take us down to Haweswater Reservoir.

Wainwright had written of Kidsty Pike, *"its summit is the best station for taking a last long look at the serrated mountain skyline of Lakeland, the like of which will not be seen again this side of the North Sea. But there will be other years, other visits. The hills will wait."*

Having eaten little so far, it seemed a good opportunity for lunch. We sat down against a low cairn, which provided scant protection from the wind and unwrapped our sandwiches. Suddenly the clouds rolled in, enveloping us. All visibility was lost. Hurriedly we stashed our food inside our packs and scrambled back to the track that had brought us here. In our panic we took one of the other tracks and it was only by checking the compass that we found the right path.

With minimum visibility, we kept our eyes trained on the rocky path at our feet and followed it down. Ten minutes later we were below the clouds and could see our surroundings again. It was a very steep descent that seemed to go on forever and I kept looking back to our cloud covered picnic spot on Kidsty Pike. It was amazing how different I felt when I lost my bearings, and how important the map and compass were.

Down at the perimeter of the Haweswater Reservoir we followed a track, which loosely followed the water's edge. In 1930, the Manchester Corporation Water Works flooded the valley to make a large reservoir for the city's water supply and drowned the villages of Mardale and Measand. During severe droughts, the water level falls to a point where the ruined buildings of the villages are visible and souvenir hunters manage to cart away some of the old village stones. The Manchester Corporation had promised to build a good walking track alongside the newly created reservoir as part compensation for the flooding, but the track was rough and uncomfortable, absolutely no compensation for us!

Haweswater was four miles long and somewhat of a dreary walk after the day's adventures on the high fells. Onwards we plodded, the fight taken out of us after the hasty departure from Kidsty Pike. Thankfully we came to the dammed end of the reservoir and walked through a small settlement called Burnbanks where we met a man who was part of a 24 hour eagle watching team. This area of Lakeland was host to the only nesting Golden Eagles in England and teams of enthusiasts maintained an around the clock vigil during the nesting season. The eagles had been lost to the area for over a century, but had returned in the early 1970s.

For the next few miles we were on a tarmac road, slowly trudging towards our night's stop at Bampton Grange. We had left Lakeland behind. I felt a mixture of sadness and relief to realise that from now on, there would be no fells to climb or lakes to walk beside. But as we were to discover, many challenges lay ahead.

The Mitre and Crown was an unusual country inn, tucked away in the small village of Bampton Grange. Across the quiet main road stood an old church whose bell marked each fifteen minute period with an appropriate gong.

We carried our packs upstairs to a bare but comfortable room. The many ascents and descents of the day, and the distances we had travelled had made us more than ready for a decent meal.

Groups of locals had already gathered in the bar downstairs, enjoying conversations over the odd pint. We ordered our meals and drinks and found a comfortable nook. During a pleasant evening we met an Australian couple also walking from Coast to Coast. John and Robyn were attempting to complete the distance in fifteen days, and judging by their athletic physiques, they would easily make it. We also met another avid eagle watcher who had taken a few days off to join his fellow eagle enthusiasts with their round-the-clock duties.

* * *

Next morning, as the church gong reminded us of the time, we set off for Orton. Since Bampton Grange was a mile or so off the official route, we made our way along the public footpaths and rights of way to rejoin it via Rosgill. Crossing over the bridge at the Lowther River, we followed the path through a field in which Goodcroft House stood. This was a fine example of a long house - a design brought over by the Norsemen. It had two massive doors, one in the front wall and the other directly opposite in the back wall. With both doors opened to the wind, the Viking farmers could thresh their wheat indoors during bad weather. We still call the opening into a house, the "threshold".

A mile further on we came to the ruins of Shap Abbey, nestled beside the wooded banks of the Lowther River. We took a brief stop to admire the remains of the Abbey's tower. Refreshed, we followed a gradually ascending road to the elongated town of Shap.

For many years Shap had been a major resting place for travellers. Stagecoaches and tired horse riders would stop here overnight for a well earned rest. The A6 (Shap's high street) was a main trunk road until 1971. Many accidents had occurred on this stretch of the highway, especially in bad weather.

Since it was early afternoon, we decided to have lunch in town as a break from our usual sandwiches. There was an inviting café on the main street, ideal for such a repast.

The English couple at the next table, seeing that we were walkers were keen to talk. He was a retired magistrate who had devoted himself to good causes. His wife had enjoyed travelling with him whenever they could. They felt that England was changing too much for their liking.

After lunch we walked along the main street enjoying the lazy Saturday afternoon. I spied an old market hall, but wedged between two buildings, it seemed empty and uncared for. A sign directed the Coast to Coast walker to the left, and after following a maze of narrow lanes, we crossed a railway bridge and further on, a footbridge, which straddled the busy M6 motorway.

Standing on the footbridge, I mused at the traffic speeding by underneath. We're all in a hurry to get somewhere; sometimes even the walker. Rebecca Solnit had written in her book, "Wanderlust: A history of Walking", that she loved walking because it was slow. "I suspect that the mind, like the feet, works at about three miles an hour. If this is so, then modern life is moving faster than the speed of thought, or thoughtfulness."

On crossing the M6 I knew that we had covered a third of our journey. From this noisy vantage point, I could just make out the last of the Lakeland peaks in the hazy distance.

Away from the motorway, we reached a quieter countryside. The landscape was populated with limestone outcrops, which added solidity to the green hills.

The area had a melancholic and lonely feel about it. Even the sun seemed subdued, somehow softened by the afternoon haze; fleeting shadows adding to the ethereal ambience. We ascended the rolling hills to the secluded hamlet of Oddendale, partially hidden by a copse of trees and a protective wall. It felt appropriate not to venture in, and in any case I was keen to visit the stone circle nearby.

I had to look carefully to find the sacred arrangement of stones. Reaching it; we sat down for a quiet contemplation. A deep silence settled over the circle, the gentle sun warming us. Carol nestled against one of the stones and snoozed. I closed my eyes and let a myriad thoughts wash over me. I had the sense of slowly being swallowed up by the land, never to be seen again. We enjoyed the serenity of the circle. Eventually, noting the time, we hoisted our packs onto our backs and regained the track.

The bleaker moorland ahead was studded with more of the weathered limestone outcrops we had seen earlier. Walking along a small valley floor we came across a cairn of rocks known as Robin Hood's Grave. England was studded with places bearing Robin's name. This cairn was unlikely to be his actual grave, but was a reminder that we still had many miles to walk before we reached Robin Hood's Bay. As we wound our way through tough, knee-high heather, the quietness of the countryside was punctuated by a shrill sound. Just ahead was a man blowing a whistle.

"That's an interesting bird sound." Carol teased him.

"Oh, I'm trying to coax one of my dogs back from the fields. He's got his nose on something and he's not keen to come," he replied.

After some time the dog did return. Rastus was a lively young dog and was happy to rejoin his master and the other dog, a Border Collie. Henry, the whistle owner, was a retired teacher who lived in Orton, where we were to spend the night. Companionably we ambled with Henry towards Orton. The fields were lush with moist grass and the attractive village with its Tudor church tower was easily visible down in the valley ahead of us.

On the way Carol questioned Henry about the etiquette of walking through fields.

"We've been keeping to the walls in case we scare the sheep or cattle."

"No need to do that," Henry advised, "you can walk in a straight line from one stile to another. In England we have an old tradition called 'Right of way', which we zealously guard."

Henry bade us farewell when we reached Orton and we headed towards the George Inn.

The Search for Balder

EHWAZ
(progress)

The gods did not kill Hoder because violence was forbidden within the boundaries of Asgard. So they confined him to one of the palaces, while Balder's spirit made the quick journey to Niflheim, the Land of the Dead

Having heard the gods' laments, Frigg hurried over to their circle, only to find her son dead. She begged the gods to go to Niflheim and ask Hel for Balder's return, because the earth would not easily exist without him.

As the way to the Land of the Dead was dangerous for any living being, no-one stepped forward, so Frigg announced, "Whoever brings Balder back will be well rewarded."

Hermod, Balder's youngest brother, stepped forward and accepted the challenge. Odin even let him use his eight-legged horse, Sleipnir to help him travel faster. Hermod and Sleipnir set out on the dark and dangerous road to Niflheim.

The gods were left to organise Balder's funeral. Odin oversaw the preparations for the pyre on Balder's ship. The gods went into the forest and cut down great pines for the occasion. Once the pyre was assembled, the fearsomely attractive Valkyries dressed the dead god in full attire. His helmet with the wings of clear thought was placed on his head, the sword of clear intentions by his side and his sandals of clear movement on his cold feet.

One by one the gods paid their respects. Balder's widow, Blossom, her heart broken, fell onto the pyre and was laid alongside her dead husband. His horse and hounds were slain and laid next to him. In deep sorrow, the gods heaped their precious possessions around Balder's body.

Odin came last and lamented over his dead son, his empty eye socket a vivid gash of emotional pain. He gave the signal for the pyre to be lit. The fire began to take. The pine cones crackled in the intense heat. A strong scent of pine resin permeated the air as the fire engulfed Balder's earthly remains. The gods tried to launch the fiery vessel, but due to the weight of their offerings, they could not budge it. The Frost Giants had been observing the funeral proceedings and because they too loved Balder, assisted their arch enemies in launching the vessel. The fiery vessel floated out upon the sea towards the horizon. As it drew nearer to the line which separated the sea from the sky, the flaming pyre sank beneath the waters and the world was left in darkness.

The gods returned to Asgard, their hearts filled with an unfamiliar foreboding. Odin himself was very concerned. The Fates had prophesied that his son's death was the first sign of the approaching Doom.

Meanwhile Hermod, riding upon Odin's steed, approached the black river which separated the dark realm of Niflheim from the world of the living. Horse and rider crossed the bridge and were challenged by a huge dog.

The dog asked Hermod, "why do you, a living man, seek access to Niflheim? Only the dead are allowed here." So the youngest god explained his quest to find his brother.

He then asked the dog, "Have Balder and his wife passed here?" The dog confirmed that such a party had recently arrived via the Hel-gate.

Hermod and Sleipnir continued and soon entered Hel's great hall where they found a pale Balder and a withered Blossom. The young brother urged them to accompany him back to Asgard.

Balder replied, "Unless you can persuade Hel to release us, we must remain here until the final day."

Hermod sought an audience with Hel and begged her to give up Balder and Blossom. The queen of the underworld listened quietly and then spoke.

"I will release Balder on one condition."

"What is it?" cried Hermod, hope growing.

"All things on earth must show their sorrow at Balder's death by weeping," she proclaimed. "If you show me this, then Balder and Blossom will be free to return."

Hermod was overjoyed. Here was a chance to obtain the release of his kinfolk. He shared his excitement with the two prisoners and quickly returned to Asgard with the news.

The gods were encouraged and sent emissaries around the world to gather confirmation of the world's sadness at Balder's death. And much evidence did they find. Tears fell from plants and leaves, even metals and stones wept with the morning dew. The world indeed grieved for Balder.

As the emissaries made their way back to Asgard, they saw an old crone sitting in a dark cave. They asked her if she would shed a tear for Balder. She answered with a sneer, "Balder did me no good while he was alive and now that he's dead, I shall not weep for him. Let Hel keep him." And the crone fled further into the darkness of her cave. The emissaries returned dejectedly to Asgard with the terrible news.

The gods knew that there was only one being who would purposely hinder Balder's return. The old crone must have been Loki in disguise. This was the last straw. The gods decided to capture Loki and imprison him forever, where he could do no further harm.

Thor led the search. Loki knew that the gods would try and hunt him down. He had finally and irrevocably overstepped the mark. Changing into a bird, he flew off and found a small house near a stream and hid there. It had four entrances, so that he could make a quick escape through one of them if he needed. Heimdall put his extraordinary senses to work and was soon able to discern the beating heart of a worried bird. He led Thor and the other gods towards the dwelling. As the gods approached the house Loki exited and dived into the water where he changed into a fish and hid behind a rock. Thor waded into the stream, looking for his prey. Loki began swimming away, but with a quick thrust of his arm, Thor tightly grasped the fish's tail, almost breaking its bones.

He had Loki. The troublemaker was forced to change back into his usual shape and the gods bound him. They dragged him off to the deep chasm in which they had already imprisoned Fenris the wolf. They firmly chained Loki to the rock floor alongside Fenris. Here he would cause no more trouble.

⊕ To Kirkby Stephen

Sunday morning. The village of Orton lay quietly warmed by a gentle sun. Surprisingly, I found I was disappointed with the weather. I had read so much about the miserable conditions experienced by other walkers on the journey that I felt I was missing out on something. Carol did not share my disappointment.

"The weather has been a pleasant surprise. You'd better be careful about what you wish for," she cautioned.

I snapped out of such ridiculous thinking and began appreciating the weather that we had been granted. After all, it must have been a record to have this much (seven days) continuous sunshine on the Coast to Coast walk.

We made our way along the road, leaving Orton behind. We briefly stopped and looked at another stone circle known locally as the Druidical Temple. The track now led through open fields and we could see more of the massive limestone outcrops on our left. We separated here and walked at our individual paces.

Quietly progressing across the fields, I again appreciated being able to walk solo for a while. The chirping and aerial manoeuvres of a skylark accentuated the openness of this wide and pleasant countryside.

I passed the small settlement of Sunbiggin and then crossed fields which would have been very boggy had there been any rain. A road separated the fields from Sunbiggin Tarn, a large reedy pond that attracted a profusion of birds. I could see a bird watchers' hut on the far side. The melancholy screeching of gulls reminded me of the seaside we had left behind at St Bees a week ago.

Carol wasn't too far behind, and we met for lunch together near the tarn.

The fare was cheese and pickle sandwiches, an apple and a fruit drink. We squirreled away some fruitcake for later, in case of afternoon hunger pangs.

There were another nine miles of walking before reaching the town of Kirkby Stephen. We followed the tarred road for the next two miles, until the path veered off to the left and tracked along the high ground above the lovely Smardale Valley. We descended and came across a disused railway. The metal rails had been removed long ago and the gentle gradients now attracted weekend walkers. The Smardalegill Viaduct looked very smart in the distance.

At the bottom of the valley we crossed the Smardale Bridge, and began the ascent up the other side. There were a number of raised mounds known as Giants' Graves nearby. Every country has legends of giants and I had often wondered which kernel of truth had produced such myths.

From here the countryside continued to be lush and green and the sun beckoned us to continue to the outskirts of Kirkby Stephen.

We followed the track that led along a back lane and out onto the long main road of Kirkby Stephen. There was our accommodation, perched right on the main street. The "Jolly Farmer" was a comfortably renovated inn. The assortment of boots and walking staves in the corridor suggested that this was a popular walkers' overnight spot. After a shower and afternoon tea, we walked into the centre of the town.

The name Kirkby Stephen was derived from Old Norse and English words meaning "a settlement with a church of St Stephen". Throughout our journey, we had come across a number of Norse and Anglo-Saxon legacies and I was fascinated to discover how much of our present is still influenced by the past.

The church tower was visible from a distance and added to the character of the town. Georgian and Gothic buildings lined the main street, which led to the centre of the town with its market place and Church of St Stephen.

An elegant gateway to the church grounds faced the market square. We passed beneath the columns of the gateway and walked over the weatherworn flagstones. Tall trees lined the pathway to the entrance of St Stephen's Church.

As we walked through the porch door and stepped into the baptismal area

I felt an electric tingle all over my skin. Immediately in front of us was a large stone carving depicting a horned and bearded man whose arms and legs were bound to a rock. A vase of gladioli placed next to the figure softened the harshness of the stonework. The figure imprisoned in the stone was Loki, the Old Norse god, one of the earliest Christian symbols of the devil in human shape. This Teutonic concept had been spread across Europe by invaders and settlers from the north. The explanation on the inscription at its base also mentioned that this particular work was one of only two extant examples in Europe.

THE LOKI STONE KIRKBY STEPHEN

Inside the large church were all sorts of interesting artifacts and nooks that caught my eye. The pulpit was made from Shap granite, and above the Hartley Chapel was an engraved panel showing the stoning of St Stephen.

This site had been a place of worship since 900AD when the Saxons first built a church here. The Normans later rebuilt it and eventually a Tudor tower was added, similar to the one we had seen at Shap Abbey.

There were stone ledges that protruded from the interior walls. I had seen these in the other churches we had visited in the course of our walk. In medieval times there were no pews or seating for the congregation and people had to stand throughout the service. Those who were ill or had difficulty in standing would "go to the wall" to sit down.

The 18th century bread shelves attached to the rear nave pillars were once used to distribute bread to the poor. A mass was being celebrated in the Hartley chapel, so we quietly walked around and continued admiring the church's interior.

We had been looking forward to a meal at Kirkby Stephen's Coast to Coast Fish Shop - a favourite of Wainwright's but were disappointed to find it closed.

Walking back through the town we peeked into a few places that were serving food but found nothing tempting.

OK, so dinner at the Jolly Farmer's it was to be. While we waited with our pre-dinner drinks in the bar room, two talkative women with North American accents arrived and sat at a nearby table. We got to chatting and decided to dine together.

And what a delightful evening it turned out to be. Connie and Caroline had left their families back in Canada to fend for themselves and flew across the Atlantic to do the walk. They joked about how they found most of the walkers they had met "destination driven", while the two Canadians enjoyed "being driven to their destination" - if the opportunity arose. They recounted an incident in which they had met a young cyclist who had stopped to chat and in the conversation Connie mentioned that they were fairly tired and hoped that their B&B was close by. The young man had offered to double them on his bike and added he was sorry, but he couldn't manage their packs as well!

They were here to have a good time and if the night's hilarity and good humour were any indication, their intentions were being fulfilled.

* * *

Another beautiful day began as we crossed over "Frank's Bridge", beneath which the Eden River flowed, and sauntered out of town. From there we faced a steep ascent. We passed by the blooming, multi-coloured poppies growing in the carefully tended gardens of the Hartley cottages. In local folklore the shimmering red poppies symbolized the ultimate sleep of death. Leaving behind the large, dusty quarries and the gorse-bush lane, we came out upon Hartley Fell and found the briskness of the headwind unpleasant. I had never thought of England as being a windy country, but so often we kept encountering headwinds.

Wainwright said that one of the reasons he had chosen an easterly crossing of England was because the wind would be at the walker's back, but it had been blowing in our faces from the day we left St Bees. I put this wind factor down to the unusually fine weather we had been experiencing. Notwithstanding my previous thoughts about missing out on wet weather, I accepted that I would rather face the wind than have to go sploshing along muddy tracks in pouring rain.

Stopping on the ascent to grab our breaths, we turned to look at the panorama behind us. A lovely haze softened any indication of modern towns or industry. We continued the steady climb and half a mile later crossed over Faraday Gill, associated with the Faraday family, whose gifted son, Michael, had been a pioneer in electrical research. Further on was a signpost, which showed the seasonal routes. The authorities, mindful of the increasing erosion caused by the ever growing hordes of walkers, had devised alternative paths to spread the wear and tear across several routes. We were to follow the red one.

Occasionally, we glimpsed a group of tall cairns known as the Nine Standards. No-one really knows who built them or for what reason, but one story was that they were placed on this Pennine ridge to give the marauding Scots the impression that here were able folk, always ready to defend their lands from unwelcome interlopers. Another theory held that it was associated with the Norse usage of the numeral nine, which was significant in their mythology. The Nine Standards were certainly old, being recorded on maps dating from the 18th century when detailed charts of the area were being produced.

We kept climbing through the sparse clumps of heather interspersed with peat soil. Thin wisps of clouds streaked the blue sky.

"The Nine Standards appeared in all their glory..."

Just after a particularly steep climb, the Nine Standards appeared in all their glory. Their construction was clearer to see as we approached them. Thousands of thick sheets of slate and granite pieces had been painstakingly placed together to form tall cairns. Originally nine had been built, but over time people had added extra ones.

There was even a comfortable bench, constructed to lessen the ferocity of the wind, on which to have lunch. We were indeed lucky to be here on such a fine day. This was the northern most summit of the Pennine Dales, the range that formed the spine of Northern England. From here water flowed westwards to the Irish Sea and eastwards to the North Sea. At this junction, the Coast to Coast walk and the Pennine Way met and crossed. Wainwright had walked the Pennines and compared them with the Coast to Coast walk in his personal notes; *"I finished the Pennine Way with relief, the Coast to Coast Walk with regret. That's the difference."*

Down below was the Eden Valley and all around were magnificent views that stretched towards the far off horizon. The Eden River snaked lazily along the valley floor. Wordsworth had discovered the Eden Valley late in life, and was inspired to pen,

"For things far off we toil, while many a good,
Not sought because too near, is never gained."

The air was fresh and clean and so invigorating to suck up through one's nostrils and exhale heavily through the mouth.

From the top of England, we began a gradual descent along White Mossy Hill. Here were peat bogs without end. Border signs indicated that we had left Cumbria and entered Yorkshire, which had often been referred to as God's own Country. A wild and bleak landscape lay before us. There was a well worn meandering path that led a long way down to the Pillar at Millstones.

I was some distance down the track when I heard a yell and turned around to see what had happened. Carol was waving for me to stop. She was sitting on the ground nursing her knee. I walked back up the slope to see what had happened.

"I stepped onto a patch of grass and my foot just sank into it," she said with a mixture of exasperation and mournfulness. "And then with my next step going down into more mud, I wrenched my knee getting out. I just hope I haven't torn anything."

I relieved her of her daypack and we continued slowly and haltingly down to the Pillar, a tall stone marker. A rest was required. We sat down with our backs resting against the sun-warmed rocks. Our spirits soon revived after sipping some water and sharing a Mars Bar. We set off again. Carol's knee was very sore, but she could walk on it carefully as long as she had no load to carry.

The path remained close to the tinkling sound of Whitsundale Beck, and as the moors were riddled with peat bogs, we took extra care walking around any suspect mud patches. We made our way down to the small settlement of Ravens Seat, situated at the bottom of a valley and entered an area redolent with names from Viking times.

Ravens Seat derived from *Hrafn's Saetr* - Hrafn's hill pasture settlement. The track led further to where Whitsundale Beck joined the Swale River and we crossed another bridge to continue walking on a tarred road. The river had cut its way through the limestone strata and left Cotterby Scar as a reminder of the power of flowing water over eons of time.

A road sign showing Keld to be a quarter of a mile away, stood out like a welcome beacon. Our muscles started to relax in anticipation of a rest. It was the longest quarter of a mile in Britain. Before I could start complaining, the little village of Keld appeared over the crest and we found our way to Butt House, our accommodation that night.

Doreen Whitehead was a no nonsense type of woman who made us welcome and showed us our room. We were then invited into the cosy lounge room to join another couple for afternoon tea. Home made cakes and delicious tea for walkers. And pleasant company as well.

Ken and Jen, walkers from Manchester, were on a circular walk via Keld and had stayed with Doreen before. Doreen was fascinating to listen to, as she related various anecdotes of life in Keld. Three younger walkers arrived and introduced themselves. Doreen asked whether they would be eating in, but they had plans that night to visit Tan Hill, England's highest inn.

Eventually everyone left the lounge room to attend to other duties so I was left to my self, which suited me fine. Doreen and husband Ernest had a remarkable library stocked with all sorts of background reading material on the local area and walks, which I ploughed into.

Before I knew it, dinner was ready so we sat down at the table. The tasty food was served with a smooth white wine. Over dinner the four of us found that we had all walked the pilgrimage path to Santiago de Compostela in Spain, so the conversation was flavoured by memories of shared experiences. The path to Santiago stretched across Europe and was first opened up for pilgrims wishing to make the long journey to the tomb of St James in the north west corner of Spain.

Doreen joined us later and spoke of her acquaintance with Wainwright whom she had first met many years ago. He had encouraged her to set up accommodation for walkers in Keld. She was also a friend of William Hague, the current leader of the Opposition. She told us that on his occasional visits to Butt House, he would spend his time in the kitchen with herself and Ernest, while the paying guests enjoyed their evening in the lounge room unaware of their close proximity to the Tory leader.

Although the young folk had not yet returned from Tan Hill, I outstayed the others, engrossed in the local literature, and eventually turned in near midnight. Before succumbing to sleep, it occurred to me that we had reached the halfway point of our walk!

AD 793
The First Viking Raids

In 793, the Anglo-Saxon augurs and soothsayers began seeing "fiery dragons in the sky". Other omens of disaster were also noticed. Reports of blood dripping from the holy church in Earowic (Anglo-Saxon York) were plentiful. All the portents suggested that some terrible calamity was about to be visited upon the hard-pressed peoples living on the island.

* * *

The Vikings from the frozen north attacked. In that year of 793, Vikings raided the monastery at Lindisfarne, where the church plate and various ecclesiastical pieces made rich pickings. After killing a number of monks, the Vikings abducted the remainder and carried them off with their loot. The Church was aghast. The Holy Island of Lindisfarne had been considered sacrosanct and inviolable.

VIKING RAIDS

"How dare these heathen raiders despoil us so," the shocked Church leaders exclaimed. The raiders returned to the monastery at Jarrow the following year with similar results. The monasteries had been easy pickings. Many of the forts and monastic centres were built on isolated coastlines and thought to be unassailable. The Vikings challenged those assumptions and showed that a determined band of marauders could quickly land their shallow craft and attack these strongholds with little warning. Viking attacks increased in frequency, usually causing havoc amongst coastal communities, but occasionally resulting in Viking losses.

The black hulled longboats ploughed through the grey green seas, weathering the storms and bleak conditions of the North Sea. These vessels were designed with a shallow draft, enabling the pirates to skim the seas quickly and maneouver along shallow rivers. The boats had two prows, to enable quick reversals when required. The versatility and manoeuverability of their vessels gave the Vikings the great advantages of speed and stealth; taking the European kingdoms by surprise. Augmenting the power of a main sail with a crew of strong oarsmen, the longboats travelled swiftly. A carving of a sacred dragon or a snarling creature on the prow of each vessel intensified the sense of a powerful alignment with the raw elements of the world. The average ship had a crew of thirty men who had been chosen for their strength in rowing and weaponry skills. Strict regulations were enforced. Quarrelling was forbidden on board and all plunder was divided among the crew according to predetermined rules. As the raiding vessels journeyed through the cold seas, the Vikings knew that their destiny was to take advantage of the world around them; the behaviour of their gods had made that clear to them. Death was less important to them than the sagas their *skalds* (storytellers) would tell their families and fellow warriors of their brave exploits.

The oarsmen were kept refreshed by the strong tang of salt spray. The grey clouds seemed to scrape the tops of the waves. These pirates were inured to such conditions, having experienced excruciatingly cold winters in their northern homelands.

It was nearing sunset as the longboats approached the shoreline. The men on board had prepared themselves for the raid on the settlement perched up on the cliffs. Each man was armed with a sword and dagger, and all were within easy reach of a dangerous arsenal of double-bladed axes. The breaking waves dumped cold water into the open vessels, which was then scooped up with wooden utensils and thrown back into the sea.

As the blood red sun dipped below the horizon, the temperature plummetted, helping steel the raiders for their purpose. Vikings usually travelled in larger groups, but this time they reckoned that the villagers would offer little resistance, and decided that three raiding vessels of men would be a sufficient force for the night's plundering.

Bihorik, chief of these raiders, had given the signal to stealthily approach the mouth of the river. The vessels were manoeuvered along the narrow river and quickly beached. Making little noise, the men climbed over the sides and stepped onto the stony bank. The village was located up on the wooded slope. There was no indication that anyone had detected them. It was unusual that they heard no sounds from the village. The Vikings quickly made their way up into the wooded area.

Suddenly, there was an explosion of screams and the brandishing of fire torches. Dry straw around them was being set alight. Flashes from the fire glinted from numerous metal blades as the Saxon villagers ran screaming at the intruders. In the fading light, now disrupted by the flaming spot fires, the Saxons began thrusting swords into the bodies of the surprised raiders. One defender sliced straight through a raider's thigh, who toppled over, surprised at the loss of balance. Firebrands were hurled, searing flesh and setting hair, clothes and animal furs alight. Wounded men howled in agony.

As the Vikings recovered from the unexpectedly strong resistance, the Saxons began to experience some of the renowned Norse warfare as the raiders cut their way up into the Saxon throngs. Double-edged axes cut through bone and skull as easily as through wood. The screaming and howling continued but the raiders were not advancing and it appeared that more Saxons were joining in the battle. Bihorik quickly assessed the situation; somehow the Saxons had known of the raid and had prepared themselves. He decided that this was not to be their night and gave the signal for his men to return to their longboats.

The Saxons, seeing the enemy retreat, smelt victory and gave chase. Rocks and knives were thrown at the fleeing raiders, badly injuring some of them. Bihorik was hit in the back by an airborne sword and toppled over. His men grabbed him and dragged him the short distance to the boats. Already two of the vessels had started to move out along the river. Vikings in the third vessel hurriedly cast off, accompanied by a shower of rocks, spears and insults.

The Vikings made their way back to the safety of the sea and followed the coastline northwards until they reached a secluded bay, which they knew was secure and there they beached.

Bihorik and some of his men were mortally wounded, but still alive. Some of the wounds were horrendous, limbs half cut away, severe head injuries and worrisome burns. Most of the wounded would not see the night out.

Bihorik breathed his last words to Gunnar and Hrafn, his kinfolk, "Put me in a ship and push it out to sea."

The remaining Vikings prepared a funeral pyre for him. They selected the least sea-worthy longboat for the platform and placed pieces of driftwood and any other flammable materials they could find, into it. Then they lifted the bodies of their dead fellow warriors and placed them aboard. They clothed Bihorik in his finest raiments and placed his corpse in the centre of the boat. Finally, they positioned his war helmet on his head and placed his sword, daggers and axe by his side.

Meanwhile, two men using flints and fine dry materials created a small fire. The fire was transferred to larger torches and applied to the kindling on board.

The dead men, who had travelled here from the land of frost and ice, were now going to pass through the threshold of fire to meet their gods. As the fire began to take, it provided an eerie glow to the sands of the narrow beach. The shadows cast by the steadily growing firelight moved about tremulously against the illumined cliff walls. It was a Viking belief that slain warriors would be chosen by Odin the Allfather and his Valkyries and taken to a fabulous place called Valholl. There they would continue to battle and feast until they were called to join the gods in the final battle against their enemies.

A black shape suddenly swooped down out of the darkness and alighted on Bihorik's corpse, undeterred by the flames licking around it. The Vikings were not surprised that a raven had arrived at this solemn time. Ravens were a symbol of the Allfather, and the Norse raiders could expect the chieftain of the gods to visit the glorious dead on such an occasion.

The large raven located a metal disk, chained around Bihorik's neck, and began to tug at it with its beak. The men looked at the raven with wonder. Here was Odin's messenger at work. The raven managed to twist the disk free, clasped it in its strong beak and hopped around on the chief's corpse. It slowly looked around at the circle of men with its shining black eyes, then launched itself back into the blackness of the night.

⊕ Along the Swale

We woke to a foggy, misty, Keld morning. Had the weather finally turned bad? In such conditions, Wainwright suggested that the perceptive walker should opt for the low road along the Swale River. We did not need much convincing to take the easier route today as we were both tired from yesterday's not inconsiderable climb to the Nine Standards and down to Keld, an accumulated ascent of 1900 feet over a distance of twelve miles.

A rest day would have been superb, but our timetable prevented it. At breakfast, the young folk who had made the pilgrimage to England's highest inn, didn't seem much the worse for their escapade. They told us of the grand time they had in the medieval inn and of their hair-raising minibus drive home.

After a satisfying stay at Butt House, it was time to push on, as there were eleven miles to cover today. Carol's knee injury seemed to have cleared up, but she was not taking any chances. I readjusted my pack to include her camera and water bottle. We walked the short distance back to Keld and began to follow the lovely meandering River Swale. A climb up from the Swale took us high above the river's course. By now the fog had begun to lift and we were presented with a stunning view of delightful Swaledale. From this vantage point we saw the Swale flowing languorously along the base of its ancient valley, clothed in a thin haze. The air carried a fragrant spring scent and the sun was a pale golden splodge in the sky.

Looking across the Swale valley we saw the remains of terraces built by Anglo-Saxons for the cultivation of crops, which for the most part had remained unaltered by the Vikings. However, when William the Conqueror arrived in this area, the whole of the north towards the River Tees was ravaged by his army, and most of the crops and agricultural lands were destroyed, resulting in a famine that claimed many thousands of lives.

Travelling further along the Swale, we saw small ancient settlements and stopped opposite Muker to enjoy our morning tea break. For the past few days we had journeyed through old Norse territory. The name Keld was derived from *kelda* - the Norse word for a spring. Occasionally a sign indicating a path along the river tempted us to follow it, but generally we kept to the road high above the captivating Swale valley.

The sun burnt through its hazy veil and reappeared in full strength, warming the land. The lush pastures, separated into smaller fields by old dry stone walls, gave the valley a timeless, pastoral feel. The road passed through small stone villages and we came to Gunnerside. This was undeniably Viking country. Even the inn-sign of The King's Head showed an armed Viking standing before a longboat. Gunnerside meant *Gunnar's Saetr* - Gunnar's hill pasture settlement. Gunnar and Hrafnr (from which Ravenseat derived) were probably two Norse raiders who settled in this area more than a thousand years ago.

We bought coffees from the inn and enjoyed lunch outdoors on a surprisingly comfortable wooden bench seat on the tiny village green. After lunch we continued our walk through small villages whose buildings were made of the hard stone so abundant in the area. We passed Meldecks and Low Row. The road again dipped down alongside the Swale. Carol was in a buoyant mood, pleased that yesterday's knee injury had cleared up.

We passed by Feetham Wood and continued along the Swale's flood plain. Rabbits scampered amongst the grassy verges. I had read somewhere that the

Normans had introduced rabbits into England after the invasion of 1066. The path veered away from the river to approach the town of Reeth. My knees had begun troubling me during the day and had worsened by day's end. We found our B&B and enjoyed our customary cups of tea.

That evening we slowly walked up to Reeth's large village green. The town appeared to be situated in the middle of nowhere, with a solid barrier of fells in the background. Imposing Georgian buildings, many of which were pubs, surrounded the green. The Back Bull Inn looked like the place to eat, so we walked in through the impressive entrance and found ourselves inside an atmospheric pub, with many curios placed on walls and shelves. One polished label had the pithy pronounce-

"We were presented with a stunning view of Swaledale..."

ment engraved on it:

"When all is said and done, There's more said than done!"

While getting the drinks, I asked the barman if he knew the origin of the name "Reeth". He said he thought it meant middle town or middle enclosure.

Just as we were preparing to leave after dinner, Neville and Judy, who we had briefly met at the Jolly Farmer's in Kirby Stephen, arrived, delaying our departure. Any excuse for another pint or two.

AD 836
Alfred and the Viking Scourge

At this time forests and swamplands covered much of the island. The Vikings had already journeyed far and wide seeking to assuage their hunger for wealth and land. They found the lands of the Picts and the Scots, north of Hadrian's Wall, suitable for establishing raiding bases. They were after the riches of the Anglo-Saxon lands, the wealth of its churches, its noble estates and its rich fertile lands. And they used force to obtain these riches.

The Anglo-Saxon kingdoms were evenly matched against the invaders and were able to withstand the initial onslaughts. The Vikings also attacked Ireland, establishing their main base at Dublin on the banks of the Liffey River.

During one of the Viking raids, the Anglo-Saxons of Northumbria killed the Viking leader, the legendary Ragnar "Hairy Breeches" and the raiders were put to flight. Afterwards the testy Northumbrians returned to their own intrigues.

Pirates sailing in from the northern reaches of Scotland plundered the west coast of Britain. Gaul was also a tempting prize, its northern lands easily accessible via navigable rivers.

The Anglo-Saxon leader, Egbert, based in Wessex, in the south of the island, was aiming for overall rule of the land. He was a descendent of Cerdic, who had claimed lineage back to Odin the Allfather. Gradually, with alliances and a series of successful battles, he combined the disparate kingdoms and was in a position to march on the north to bring it under his rule.

Exhausted by the bitter years of anarchy and bloodshed, the warring northern realms were no match for Egbert's armies and soon surrendered. For once, the separate kingdoms of this island began to pay allegiance to one ruler. Egbert's realm did not include the fierce Picts or Scots who inhabited the lands on the northern side of Hadrian's Wall.

Egbert, king of Wessex, a grizzled veteran who had spent most of his life fighting, died in 839, passing on the kingdom to his son Aethelwulf. The new king was a devout Christian, both blessed and burdened with a number of ambitious and capable sons, the youngest being Alfred. The House of Wessex was now predominantly Christian, tracing its ancestry back to Noah and Adam. However, in keeping with older traditions, a part of the family tree was still traceable to Odin.

Aethelwulf the new King planned a pilgrimage to Rome and temporarily left the care of his kingdom in the hands of his oldest son, Aethelbald. Accompanied by his youngest son Alfred, the King travelled to Rome, where Alfred was presented to the pope. The King and young Alfred returned via the land of the Franks, where Aelthelwulf married Judith, daughter of Charles the Bald. Upon Aethelwulf's return to Wessex, Aethelbald opposed his father's resumption of kingship. The king yielded Wessex to his ambitious son. The people did not take to Aethelbald because he openly flouted traditions. He was eventually succeeded by his brother, Aethelred who became king in 866.

* * *

Later that year, more black-hulled Scandinavian ships reached the south-eastern shores of the island and the invaders began their desecration and plunder of the towns.

The "Great Army" from Denmark had arrived in East Anglia and began destroying many of the island's kingdoms. The Danes attacked villages and towns, slaughtering the men, raping the women or selling them into slavery. Children were tossed onto spikes or forced into slavery. Christian priests were slain in the name of Odin and Tew. Barbarism and chaos reigned again.

Although the Anglo-Saxon and Viking religions originated from the same root beliefs, the Vikings had had three more centuries of relative isolation in which to develop their mythology. The Anglo-Saxon religions had many aspects in common with the earlier pre-Roman Celtic religions as well as with Viking beliefs.

The "Great Army" was led by the sons of the Viking Ragnar "Hairy Breeches" who had been captured and slain by the Northumbrians. His sons, Halfdan, Ubbi and Ivar the Boneless, were spoiling for revenge and were intent on avenging their father's death by annihilating the Northumbrians.

The Danes made a quick peace treaty with King Edmund of East Anglia, comandeered all available horses and advanced towards Northumbria in a foul mood. They savaged the ancient Roman town of Eboracum, which the Anglo-Saxons called Earowic, and renamed it Jorvik. The Danes set up camp behind Jorvik's old Roman walls. They then set about slaughtering the Northumbrians. As this did not sate their bloodlust, they marched upon Nottingham, but the Saxons managed to blockade them there. A peace was negotiated which allowed the Danes to return to Jorvik unmolested.

In 870 the Danes attacked East Anglia and tortured King Edmund to death. Edmund was later canonized St Edmund and the city of Bury-St-Edmunds was named after him.

King Aethelred and his brother Alfred correctly reckoned that to save Wessex, they would have to keep fighting the Danes at every opportunity, and force them to relocate.

Aethelred died and Alfred was chosen as his successor by the Witan, the group of Saxon elders. The Saxons and the Danes kept battling. In 875 the Great Army split into two segments, one moving to Northumbria to settle and the other south to Cambridge to continue raiding. It was about this time that the name Engla Lande - the land of the Angles, began to be used.

Autumn was ending and winter approached. Every year at this time, the people burnt effigies of Loki to minimise his malevolent influence during the cold months that lay ahead. Winter came and the snows fell. Harsh cold visited the land and fighting ceased. The roads were impassable and hungry wolves prowled the dense forests scavenging for food. Men and creatures settled down for the annual period of hibernation.

The Vikings had introduced the Yule feast. This celebration began on the longest night of the year, taking place during December, the month of the year considered sacred to Thor and Frey. Great feasting and rejoicing took place during this month as the Vikings celebrated the return of the sun, since every day from now on would be a little longer. The Yule was a wheel and the sun represented a golden spinning wheel in the sky. It was a Yuletide custom to burn a large log which had to last through the night. If it turned to ashes before morning, it presaged problems for the people in the New Year. The boar's head had place of honour at the feast. The boar was Frey's symbol, and at this time of year, the warriors made their vows for the coming year on a sacrificial boar.

In Cambridge, Guthrum, the wily, hardened Viking, initiated an unexpected maneouvre. In the dead of winter, he mounted an assault upon Alfred's royal residence, forcing Alfred and his family to flee for their lives. They found safety on the Isle of Athelney in the Somerset fens. The fens were vast areas of swamps and marshes that were almost impossible to navigate unless you had been raised there - as Alfred had. In Alfred's absence, Guthrum began to spread rumours that Alfred had abandoned his people and that he, Guthrum, should be their rightful ruler.

The people of Wessex became demoralised, as they did not know what had happened to their king. It was at this time, at the nadir of his reign, that Alfred wandering through the swamps, came upon a hut. Its owner, not recognising the King of Wessex, requested him to watch her cakes as they warmed over the fire. Distracted by deeper thoughts, Alfred allowed the cakes to burn thus earning himself the reputation of a bad cook. From then on things improved. Alfred converted Athelney into a fortified base and began to build up his army and carried out numerous guerrilla raids on the Danes. Every day more eager followers flocked to Alfred's side.

Alfred decided it was time to march on Guthrum's army. Totally surprised by Alfred's Lazarus-like recovery, Guthrum yielded, agreeing to the creation of a boundary between the Danes and the Saxons. He moved to East Anglia where he settled for the next decade until his death. The boundary, which stretched in a northwesterly line from London to Chester, became known as the Danelaw. The Danes controlled all the lands north of the boundary with Jorvik as its capital.

After Alfred's truce with Guthrum, life in the Danelaw gradually settled down and many of the invaders turned their energies to farming.

The Vikings brought many new words which irrevocably changed the Anglo-Saxon lexicon. In the Danelaw, words or suffixes such as by described an original Danish settlement (byr) or one now occupied by them. Kirkby was a settlement with a church.

The Viking settlers preferred to farm the hills and higher places above the forests. They introduced a lifestyle similar to that back in Scandinavia, where the mountains and valleys had provided them with a livelihood. They brought hardy sheep with them that were later called 'Herdwicks' and rotated their pastures, called saetrs. The name saetr evolved into the suffix seat or side, as in Ravenseat and Gunnerside. A temporary shelter used by shepherds was known as a *skali*, which evolved into scale.

Thwaite was a clearing or field sloping down to a valley. *Fell* (hill), *clint* (flat topped ridge), *crag* (steep rugged rock), *scar* (cliff), *beck* (brook), *gill* (narrow valley), *mere* (lake), *tarn* (small mountain pool) were all words imported from Scandinavia. So was *thorpe* (small town), *wick* (narrow opening in a field) and *toft* (site of a homestead).

Alfred was not the type to sit on his laurels. There was still too much present danger. He established a national system of local defences known as *burhs* - which became burgs or boroughs. After recapturing London from the Danes in 886, he and Guthrum signed a treaty which considered the English living in the Danelaw as equals and all Danes on English soil as people with whom Englishmen could legitimately trade. He also compiled a new code of English law and translated a number of classical Latin works into English. He undertook the task of collecting earlier texts and combined them into what became known as the Anglo-Saxon Chronicle.

Alfred's son, Edward, was from the same mould as his father. He had shown leadership in earlier battles and took up the reins of power when Alfred died. Edward knew that Wessex and the other large kingdom of Mercia would have to fight strenuously to maintain the boundary that Alfred had fought for. So he initiated the Reconquest of the Danelaw. He had the assistance of his brother-in-law, the King of Mercia. Together they kept advancing deeper and deeper into Danish territory, establishing fortified burhs as they went. They had to keep pushing until the Danes either left England or submitted to their rule.

The King of Mercia died, but his widow, Edward's sister, lent her considerable army to the effort, and earnt herself the name "Lady of the Mercians". Together the two kingdoms continued to harass and reconquer parts of the Danelaw. After the untimely death of his sister, Mercia and Wessex combined under the leadership of Edward. The relentless reconquest and consolidation of lands in the former Danelaw ended with Edward bringing into existence a United Kingdom of England.

⊕ Historic Richmond

Haughey House in Reeth was one in a row of large terrace houses near the village green. We were sitting at the dining table enjoying a Haughey House walker's breakfast when Richard, who helped run the B&B with his wife, mentioned that he was going to Richmond later that day and offered to take my pack. The Sherpa Van company was transporting Carol's pack every day and up until now I had been quite OK carrying mine. To me it was part of the walk, knowing that I had the stamina to carry my pack the distance. However with my sore knees unimproved, I relished the opportunity to walk a day without my pack, so I accepted his offer.

I put the necessities, including wet weather gear, maps and compass, into my day-pack and we set off. It was already overcast and chilly. We put on our warm clothes and goretex coats. We left Reeth through an area called Fremington. I loved the unusual names. Next came Ewelop Hill and soon after, the narrow road led us to Marrick Priory with its impressive tower. The priory was founded in the twelfth century to accommodate Benedictine nuns and was now used as a residential youth activity centre.

Just past the priory we entered Steps Woods, which incorporated the delightful Nun's Causey or Walk, which still linked the priory to the village of Marrick, a mile away.

There was no mistaking the biting cold of the day. Stopping briefly at Marrick, we added more layers of clothes beneath our goretexes. The layout of the village was confusing and we took a wrong turn, but soon retraced our steps and found the right way. We followed the track down through ancient fields and over solid stiles. I felt we were out in the middle of nowhere. Again I became aware of the persistent cold wind. It always seemed to blow in our faces. Still, mustn't grumble. That particular phrase reminded me of a TV skit that Alexei Sayle, the English comedian, had once performed, lampooning the English propensity for accepting disadvantageous circumstances. And anyway, who could really complain? Walking across open fields, exercising a thousand muscles; breathing in fresh spring air laden with a hint of farmyard aroma, and generally just being in the countryside, was the stuff to bring a glowing ruddiness to one's cheeks.

We crossed the old bridge in Marske and noticed the ancient church of St Edmund just above us. A few strides further on we found ourselves back in the fields, crossing more stiles, on the track down to Clapgate Beck. From there it was a stiff climb up to Applegarth Scar. We skirted the base of neighbouring Whitcliffe Scar and continued along the track.

I had to stop to retie my boots while Carol continued. The coldness of the day was remarkable. Many trees were quite bare; magnificent skeletal structures of branches silhouetted against a pale grey sky, a stark reminder of winter's recent departure.

I continued on to a gate, which permitted access to Whitcliffe Wood and noticed two rather sorry looking walkers massaging their feet.

"Looks nasty" I prompted them.

"It's my blisters," replied the one who was applying Band-Aids to his damaged feet.

They had started their walk from Robin Hood's Bay and had been camping and sleeping in barns. The one who was repairing his blistered feet explained their condition.

"I bought these 1000 mile socks for the walk, because the makers promised that if you got blisters they would refund your money. So I'm sending them back."

Not much consolation at the moment, I thought. We wished each other well and I continued on into the woods. The road was wide and muddy, and I climbed to another gate where the woods ended abruptly. The vista opened out and I caught up with Carol. From this high vantage point, Richmond lay spread out below us with the magnificent keep of its castle visible in the distance.

We were both quite cold and ready to reach our accommodation at Richmond. For once, the wind was on our side, and pushed us along the road to the outskirts of the town. We were heading for Windsor House, our B&B, and I was ready for a right royal cup of tea. Richmond was the largest town on the Coast to Coast walk and I had been looking forward to exploring it. All roads led to the magnificent market square at the base of the dominating Norman castle and we soon found our B&B.

Windsor House was nestled in close to the walls of the castle, and our hostess Sue, made us welcome in the 400-year-old guest house, which was finished in an eclectic assortment of styles, predominantly Victorian.

Our afternoon tea ceremony gave us a chance to warm up. Then out to visit Richmond while we still had the time. By now my legs had become quite sore and I was concerned about my knees. However, I thought it was better to keep going and hope that a night's rest would rejuvenate all aching limbs. Carol had experienced no further discomfort from her knee and led the way into town.

Richmond's heart, the interesting market square, lay outside the castle walls. Here we were in an ancient setting, with the shops and old stone buildings shoulder to shoulder around the perimeter of the market place. Even the minibuses, ready to ferry passengers to the suburbs or further afield, did not detract from the overall medieval impression. Richmond meant strong or rich hill. We were in the original Richmond. There were at least 56 other places around the world named Richmond.

The first matter of business was to visit the castle. Situated on the highest point in the old town, it had been constructed as an impregnable fortress by Alan Rufus (Alan The Red), who had served in the Breton contingent of William the Conqueror's army at the battle of Hastings. Rufus was a solid supporter of the conqueror and consequently was granted ownership of more than four hundred manors across Yorkshire and Lincolnshire. Immense stone walls protected the vast castle grounds. I wondered what the view from the tower was like.

Carol stayed below while I climbed the stairs to the top of the magnificent keep, looking at the restored interiors at each level. At the top, I followed the square walkway around the battlements and was pleased that the views were worth the climb. Looking down below at the market place, I half closed my eyes, and easily imagined a medieval town, with its inhabitants going about their business.

The Swale, which flowed around the base of the castle and out beneath Richmond Bridge, looked grey and cold under the darkening sky. I climbed down the narrow stone stairwell and we left the castle grounds to explore the other parts of old Richmond.

Richmond's narrow lanes were called Wynds, and there was even one named after St James of Compostela. From the signs denoting local place names, such as Temple Gardens and Temple Terraces, it seemed that the Templars had had a significant presence here in the past. The Templars were warrior monks who protected pilgrims journeying to Christian shrines in medieval times. We found a pleasant café in Frenchgate and enjoyed a simple dinner.

Thor and the World Serpent

LAGU
(water)

While the rest of the gods had become reflective after Balder's death, Thor was unable to sit still. It was not that he had no heart for what had happened. The truth was, he was addicted to action and best of all, and he loved to fight giants and monsters. Some time ago he had got it into his head to capture and kill the Serpent which lay quietly coiled around the world beneath the sea. Thor knew that to disturb the serpent would create worldwide upheavals, but nevertheless his mind was made up and he set out upon the hunt. He travelled for a long time and one day came upon Hymir, a giant who was skilled in fishing and bred cattle in his spare time. Thor sheltered under Hymir's roof for a night and in the morning asked if he could join the giant in his daily fishing. Hymir did not recognise Thor as one of the gods and was reluctant to take this young man along with him.

Thor asked what type of bait he should use. The giant insulted him by replying, "What sort of fisherman are you? Work it out for yourself."

Thor restrained himself from letting Hymir feel the full force of his hammer. Instead, he grabbed one of the giant's bulls and wrenched its head off, throwing it into the boat. "That will do as bait," Thor informed the giant. Hymir's jaw dropped in astonishment.

They set off across the sea and Hymir was impressed by the young man's rowing ability. Thor continued to row out to sea further than the giant had ever been, to the spot where the World Serpent was likely to be. Thor fastened the bull's head to the line and threw it into the water. The bull's head sank further and further into the dark sea. The Serpent smelt the pungent morsel and grasped it in its jaws. The line grew taut and Thor was drawn to the edge of the boat. He managed to reel in the line and half hoist the Serpent into the boat. Thor and the serpent looked with fury at one another and the Serpent spat venom at him. The terrified Hymir managed to cut the line, releasing the Serpent back into the water where he quickly returned to the bottom of the ocean. This whole episode had set off tidal waves and geological convulsions around the globe. Thor had made an enemy of the sea creature.

⊕ A Danish Settlement by the River

Brrr, another cold day. Inside Windsor House at Richmond it was comfortably warm, and a pleasant surprise of smoked salmon and eggs awaited us for breakfast. I took the opportunity to read the morning paper. There was an article about the sale of the Rover Motor Company. I noticed that Rover's insignia was a Viking longboat under full sail! What a legacy those ancient raiders had left.

Carol, who had developed a heavy cold overnight had bought herself a copy of a book by Yorkshire vet, James Herriot, whose BBC TV series had been filmed in this area, in the Oxfam shop. She rang ahead to The White Swan at Danby Wiske to let the owners know that she would be arriving early. She then cheerfully boarded a bus and once at The White Swan, spent the rest of the day reading in bed. I would have the day to myself, walking the fourteen easy miles to meet her there that afternoon.

Today's walk was through the Vale of Mowbray. The map indicated easy, flat country walking, mostly along the Swale, including a few miles on roads. I was confident I would make good time.

On my way out of Richmond, following the guidebook's clear instructions, I passed the walls of the old castle and a sewage plant before reaching a small wood. The path was quite muddy. Next came the small hamlet of Colburn where I lost my way and had to back track. The fields ahead were green and lush. Soon, I heard the muffled sounds of a motorway in the distance. The meandering Swale came back into view, and I walked beneath the A1 motorway, coming out at Catterick Bridge.

There was an interesting-looking plaque on the other side of the road, so I walked over to read it. It presented a short history of the town. The early Britons had named the spot "Cataract", from the cataracts in the river. The Romans later Latinized it to Cataractonium and built a fort to patrol this section of their major north road, Dere Street. The old Roman site was now known as Catterick and was still strongly associated with the military.

I crossed the old bridge, which pre-dated the current A1 bridge, and followed the Swale along to a grassy area where I stopped for lunch. A doctor and his dog were enjoying an afternoon's walk. He told me he was between shifts at the local hospital and that he tried to get some exercise whenever possible.

Further on, where the Swale turned to the right in a majestic sweep, the path veered off in the opposite direction, taking me up to a road above a gravel works. Half a mile later I came to the quiet and secluded hamlet of Bolton-on-Swale.

The picturesque church of St. Mary was set near the centre of the village. Walking through the open wooden lych gate into the church grounds, I found a bench beneath a large yew tree. I plopped my pack on the ground and stretched out on the bench, happy to be relieved of the burden. I had seen yew trees growing in many of the church grounds we had walked past since leaving St Bees. The evergreen yew was linked to death because of its poisonous seeds and needles. It was a pre-Christian custom to plant them in graveyards. In the Middle Ages the yew was used as an antidote against enchantments, and everyone knew that the best

English longbows were made from the yew tree.

I had made good time and was in no hurry. I pondered the unusual memorial in front of me. It was constructed as an elongated pyramid set on top of a solid stone block, and commemorated the life of Henry Jenkins. He was born in 1500 and lived for an incredible 169 years, reputedly seeing or experiencing some of the events we now read about in history books. It was very pleasant just sitting there and I was reluctant to move. However the day was getting colder and I still had some miles to walk.

I left Bolton-on-Swale and followed the path along Bolton Beck to where it joined a road at Ellerton Hill. From there I continued on to the small hamlet of Streetham. At Streetham I had a choice: to cross the fields or to follow the road. Since it was only a mile to Danby Wiske from here, I chose the road and followed the sign pointing to my destination. A Landrover with the model name *Defender* embossed on its tailgate drove past, the driver nodding his head in greeting. The name Defender conjured up thoughts of past invasions of England.

It had been a good day and I was looking forward to arriving earlier than planned. I continued along the road with a smug feeling,. I had walked about a mile, but had seen no sign indicating I was getting any nearer to Danby Wiske. I looked at the map and realised that I had taken a wrong turn. A farmer was just driving out of a side road so I asked him for directions.

"Am I on the right road for Danby Wiske?"

"It's two miles up that road," he said, pointing back the way I had just walked.

My smugness evaporated and I steamed back to Streetham cursing signs and maps. I arrived at the offensive, lying, untrustworthy sign, which had pointed to Danby Wiske, and found that it was so loose that any gust of wind would have sent it pointing in any direction. My inattention to detail, and a mischievous wind had added two unnecessary miles to the day's walk. It was now very cold.

Back on the right road, I found my way to the interestingly named village of Danby Wiske. It was situated at the lowest point above sea level on our walk across England. The name *Danby Wiske* meant the settlement of the Danes by the river. Wiske or Esk was a generic term for water or a river. It was certainly a quiet and pleasant place. The village was centred on a crossroads with The White Swan and its similarly white painted neighbour being the largest buildings. A pleasant village green shaded by large trees lent it a sense of solitude.

There was no sign of life and I learned later that the innkeeper and his wife had gone out. Luckily Carol, who had spent most of the afternoon reading and sleeping, chose that moment to glance out of her window and saw me and let me in.

When Wainwright had written his guide, he had nothing good to say about the service at The White Swan,

"You might with luck, get a bag of crisps at the inn, but certainly not a meal or a sandwich," he wrote.

Since then, the inn had changed hands a number of times. The hosts, Frank and his wife, were very welcoming, and the inn seemed to be quite popular with the locals. Our room was warm and well insulated against the numbing cold outside. Obviously, things had improved since Wainwright's time.

That night we dined with Andy, a young Englishman who was also walking the Coast to Coast path. He had started his journey from Robin Hood's Bay.

"I'm planning to do it in ten days," he said.

"That's pretty solid going," I replied.

"Yes, but I was only able to get ten days leave from work and I'm really keen to finish the walk. I was planning to camp and I started off sleeping in barns, but found that too uncomfortable. I need plenty of sleep to keep up the 20 miles a day. So I'm sending the camping equipment back home and I'll stay at pubs or B&Bs for the rest of the walk," he explained

Andy was a very interesting young man. He had travelled to Australia where he had been a jackaroo and then spent some time as a student teacher in Melbourne. He had recently returned from a trek to the Mount Everest base camp, and knew a great deal about Mount Everest. We discussed Jon Krakauer's book "Into Thin Air", which told of the disastrous 1996 Everest expedition and we all agreed the Coast to Coast path was a lot more down-to-earth.

"The White Swan - things had improved since Wainwright's time..."

AD 845
The Beginnings of Normandy

The widespread Viking marauders were still on the move. They raided the countries of Fresia and Holland. In Gaul, Viking fleets sailed down the largest rivers, the Loire and the Seine, raiding the riverside towns and cities. They were attracted by the considerable amounts of valuable goods they could plunder from these large trading centres.

In 845 one Viking fleet sailed down the Seine and was stopped by two Frankish groups, which were waiting on opposite sides of the river. The Vikings attacked and defeated the smaller group, hanging the survivors. The larger group on the opposite bank saw what had happened to their fellows and lost their enthusiasm for further resistance. The raiders continued unchallenged down the Seine towards their goal - Paris.

They attacked Paris, captured and looted it. King Charles the Bald, already fully occupied with local insurrections, paid the Vikings vast amounts of silver and gold (danegeld) for them to leave Paris. Viking hordes continued to sail along the waterways, burning and pillaging. To the Christian Franks, it seemed like the apocalypse had arrived with these barbarians at the helm.

The established systems of law were breaking down all across the continent, and small centres of power were springing up. Here and there a baron would gather men loyal to him and together they would seize an area of land for themselves.

In 885, Paris was again under siege. This time the Franks controlled the Seine by fortifying the bridges, making it impossible for the Viking fleets to get close enough to the city by water. The king, Charles the Fat, also bought off the Vikings, persuading them to settle in Burgundia, where they could deal with the troublesome locals.

Some of the Viking raiders, growing old, decided to settle in Gaul. Rolf the Viking was one of these. He was known as Rolf the Ganger (walker) because he was too large to be carried by a horse, so had to walk everywhere. Early in his career, he had been exiled from Norway for stealing cattle. He had sailed off to the Orkneys where he joined up with the Viking raiding parties.

In 911, Rolf led a band of raiders and attacked Chartres in Gaul. However, the Vikings were beaten off. The Frankish King Charles the Simple, saw an opportunity to reach an agreement with his enemy, and at a hastily convened conference, agreed to cede the already occupied lands to Rolf, providing the Vikings swore allegiance to him as their king, which they did. Charles was clever, as he did not lose any extra lands, and as a bonus, he was certain that Rolf's men would act as a buffer against any further Norse attacks. The land known as Nuestria that had been ceded to the Vikings, would become Northmandy or Normandy.

AD 925
Athelstan - the Golden King

Enough! Of the fighting, pillaging and degradation of war. It was time for a period of magnificence to appear in Engla-Lande.

Athelstan, a Christian, ascended the throne of England at a time when it needed a respite from the recent decades of bloodshed. Athelstan truly looked the part of a magnificent king.

Slender and golden-haired, he graced the throne as if God had personally selected him. He was pious and greatly interested in things religious. And the holy relics he collected! In those times a collection of relics was known as a halidom and was an important part of a king's treasury. It showed that the king was pious and it also gave the ruler a set of holy artifacts upon which powerful oaths could be sworn. His obsession with relics had the favourable outcome of improving relations with the rest of Christendom and prompted a great inflow of pilgrims who journeyed to the various shrines of saints across the land. Art and culture were again encouraged.

The golden king had four beautiful sisters who were highly sought after for dynastic marriages. One sister married a Frankish Duke who brought many outstanding gifts to England. Athelstan was pleased to have the sword of Constantine the Great in his possession. The sword even had one of the nails from the Cross, set in its hilt. Another sister married the Holy Roman Emperor. The House of Wessex, the oldest royal dynasty in Europe, was again known across Europe. Tributes flowed in from his peers and things were looking up.

However, the Vikings were on the move again.

"Why couldn't they settle?" Athelstan began preparations for the likelihood of further trouble. In 927, the Norsemen in the capital of the Danelaw, Jorvik, elected Olaf as their king and he sought assistance from the Norsemen based in Dublin who were always itching to fight. Guthfrith from Dublin soon arrived to assist his allies in wresting England away from Athelstan.

The golden king advanced on Jorvik and razed the Norse defenses, scuttling the Viking dream of an Anglo-Irish kingdom. King Olaf and Guthfrith were forced to flee to Dublin. Now, perhaps those Vikings would be quiet for a while!

Athelstan ruled in the grand manner. His government, like Alfred's, understood the dual nature of the English and the Scandinavians who lived on the island and absorbed the Christian descendants of the Great Army and the Anglo-Saxon earls into a relatively acceptable mixture.

The Vikings were still a major threat and Athelstan led a combined assault on the remainder of the enemy Norsemen in a major battle at Brunanburh in 937, which routed them.

Even now, one of Athelstan's legacies remains, The Old Corporation of Malmesbury. As a reward for their help in repelling the Vikings at the battle of Brunaburgh, he granted the people of Malmesbury five hundred acres of land. The descendants of these folk conduct an annual Commoning Ceremony in which "freemen" are allowed to join this ancient community. During the ceremony, a member recites the following lines, and taps the successful applicant lightly with a twig:

"Turf and twig I give to thee,
As free as King Athelstan gave to me,
And I hope a loving brother thou wilt be."

The golden King died in 939, and was succeeded by his brother Edmund. Olaf, who had fled to Dublin, had been waiting for this chance and swiftly crossed the Irish Sea to recapture Jorvik.

Most of Edmund's time was spent dealing with the Vikings and he was killed as he went to the aid of one of his officers. His brother Eadred took his place and he in turn had his hands full curtailing the ambitious activities of the notorious Archbishop Wulfstan and Eric Bloodaxe, one of the last Viking adventurers.

Eadred set about quelling the troublesome Northumbrians once and for all. Wulfstan was put in prison and Eric was forced to live as a fugitive.

Edgar was the next notable king around 953. He earned the name of "Peaceable" because there were no external attacks on the land during his reign, so he was able to devote much of his time formalizing revisions of the law and many of the administrative sections of his position.

In 975, the "Peaceable One" died and the bishops forced his son Edward to take the throne. The clergy had become quite powerful since Athelstan's reign. The Witan didn't try hard enough to veto the Bishops' decision and rued the day Edward became king.

Edward was a self-centred, vicious teenager who was not suitable for the position. Another fiery light was seen in the sky followed shortly after by a famine. The bishops continued to support Edward, but the Witan were at their wits' end.

In 978, Edward rode unprotected into the hall at Corfe Gap to greet his mother and brother Ethelred. As he pulled on his horse's reins to stop, a number of thanes came to lend assistance to their lord. In amongst the jostling, Edward was fatally stabbed During the next few days, his younger brother Ethelred was hastily crowned king.

The nation experienced a sense of guilt at Edward's blatant murder. 'How could we so coldly kill our own King, even if he was a young n'er do well?"

The end of the millennium was approaching and with it, possibly the end of the world, a belief the Church did not dissuade. The natural disasters, the selfishness and insularity of men, war and treachery everywhere led many to believe the end was nigh. With new Viking attacks of increasing ferocity, the road to oblivion seemed close at hand.

Ethelred became an insecure ruler. Perhaps if the English could somehow redress Edward's murder then things would improve. In 979 during a national Day of Atonement, Edward's body was exhumed. The body was found to be relatively free of decay, which could only mean one thing - sainthood. He became known as

Saint Edward the Martyr.

Things didn't improve. The Vikings invaded with full-scale armies and terrorised the country. The King was saddled with treacherous advisors such as Eadric and Aelfric who said that payment of danegeld would get the invaders out of the country. This did not work. The invaders usually did their worst and were then paid a great amount of money to go home.

Ethelred may well have rued the day he became king. In a fury, possibly brought on by the frustration over a series of failed encounters with the invaders, Ethelred set about massacring the remaining Danes in England in what became known as the St. Brice's Day massacre. One of the victims was the sister of Sweyn of Denmark. Ethelred had unknowingly begun a blood feud with one of the most powerful Vikings who would be soon on his way to England for revenge and silver.

England was ripe for plunder. This was a fertile land; industrious and relatively well managed. Now with a weak and ineffectual king at its head, the country was at the mercy of the Vikings. They could plunder it and then demand payment of danegeld as a condition of departure.

Sweyn mounted raids on the coastal cities and began pillaging and looting. Under Ethelred's stewardship things grew increasingly worse.

Contemporary commentators in the Anglo-Saxon Chronicle commented that it was the combination of Ethelred and his councilors that was at fault, not just the king. They asked why the king continued to rely on proven traitors such as Eadric and Aelfric who had duped him and fought on the enemy's side before.

Meanwhile, Ethelred married Emma, daughter of the powerful Richard I, Duke of Normandy. Fortunately this gave Ethelred a family link to the growing power of the Duchy of Normandy whose nobles were carving out a place for themselves in the north of the Frankish lands.

Sweyn's series of intermittent raids over the next five years gave him the impetus to invade England. In 1009 he launched his biggest campaign with the intention of invading and settling England. The various English armies put up some isolated resistance, but without effective national leadership, had little effect against the Norse menace.

In 1013 Sweyn overran the Danelaw which marked the beginning of the end. London was still holding its own. Thanes and ealdormen throughout the country realised the futility of fighting an unwinnable war and swung across to Sweyn's side. It was their only option if they wanted to live. Only after the rest of the nation had accepted Sweyn as king did London submit. Ethelred followed his wife Emma and their princes Edward and Alfred, across the channel to exile in Normandy, where they were granted shelter in the court of Duke Robert the son of Duke Richard.

The English were left spiritless. Worse still, the Norse ruled them.

The Frost King Challenges Thor

THORN
(boundless energy)

Now that Loki had been banished from Asgard and imprisoned alongside Fenris in the deep chasm, Thor discovered that he missed the adventures that he and the arch trickster had once shared. Thor, in an uncharacteristic manner, sat down and recalled one of their old adventures.

Once again Thor was restless. He was tired of the cold blasts of wind which the frost giants sent down from the north for many months of the year. Not only were the winds unpleasant, they also caused havoc with the people's crops and killed the early tree buds. So he was off northwards to deal with the troublesome giants and in particular their king, Utgard-Loki.

Thor invited Loki to accompany him, and like Thor, Loki was always up for any adventure. They set off in Thor's chariot which was pulled by two magic goats. They travelled for many miles and that evening stopped at the hut of a peasant family. Thor had a soft spot for the common folk and enjoyed sharing meals with them.

Seeing that these folk had very little food to spare, he unhooked his magic goats and slayed them. The goats had the wonderful ability to be killed and eaten, and as long as their unbroken bones were placed inside their hides, they would miraculously recover the next morning. All had their fill that night. However Loki, unable to help himself, persuaded the peasant's son to break one of the bones and suck out its marrow. After all, this was a luxury for a peasant lad who was accustomed to eating barley and sour vegetable broth.

In the morning, Thor tapped his hammer on the hides and the goats sprang up as if from sleep. However one of them was lame. Thor looked angrily at the family and soon the son confessed. As compensation, the father offered his son and daughter in servitude, which Thor accepted.

Because the goat was lame, Thor decided to leave both goats in the care of the man and his wife and to walk with his little band.

They walked all day and that night found themselves in an unfamiliar locality enveloped in a mist. They saw a strangely shaped house and entered. Finding it dark and empty, the travellers lay down on the soft floor and went to sleep. Noisy rumblings interrupted them, and fearing that the house might collapse on top of them, they found a smaller chamber where they finally found rest.

In the morning they walked out of the chamber and discovered it was a giant's glove. The giant was just waking up. Learning that Thor and his companions were travelling to Utgard to see the frost giants, the giant accompanied them to the castle owned by Utgard-Loki, the king of the frost giants. Loki was born of a giant himself, but preferred to look like a god, hence the similarity of his name to Utgard-Loki.

They made their way into the castle and presented themselves to the giant king. Utgard-Loki recognised them and said, "I know why you have come to this castle. Let us organise some contests, and if you lose, you must leave my castle in the morning." He sat forward on his throne and added, "I have heard of your many deeds and now I would like to see them for myself."

"What's our prize for winning?" asked Loki.

"If you win, Thor may proceed with his planned destruction of my castle," the king laughed.

Wasting no time, Loki immediately bragged, "I am so hungry that I bet I can eat more than anyone here!"

Four giants carried a great trough crammed with food into the hall. Loki was placed at one end, while the castle's cook, Logi, sat at the other end. Loki proved himself and ate his way to the centre of the trough. However, his opponent had already devoured his half of the food, all the bones and the trough as well.

The king smiled and said, "Maybe there is something else that you would be better at, because eating is obviously not your strength."

Thor replied, "Bring me your biggest drinking vessel as I have a great thirst," tilting his head back in a display of bravado.

A large horn, filled to the brim was brought in. The king smirked and said, "A good drinker will finish this in one gulp, a moderate drinker in two, and a small drinker in three gulps. Let's see which one you are."

Thor raised the horn and drank. He drank and drank and drank, till he began seeing stars before his eyes and thought he would explode. The level of the liquid had only dropped a small amount. The king asked maliciously, "Since drinking is obviously not your strength either, is there any other contest in which your tiny group would care to participate?"

In front of the gods and giants, the peasant's son gathered up his courage and offered to race anyone.

The king laughed, "Young stripling, I will let you race Hugi." The race began, and although the peasant boy was strong and fleet of foot, Hugi ran like the wind and easily won the race.

Thor was at his wit's end. He was sorely tempted to use his hammer on the insulting giant, but managed to control his ire. He still had his awesome strength. So the king challenged him to pick up his cat, but Thor was only able to lift up one of its paws.

The king said, "Your prowess in these competitions has been disappointing. I thought you lot were made of stronger stuff. However, there is one final challenge left, and that is to wrestle my old nurse, Elli."

Thor, still smarting from his previous failures, settled into an arm wrestling match with the old nurse, which ended just as disastrously as the previous challenges.

The peasant girl, who had been ignored all along, whispered to Thor and Loki that she thought that the giant king was using magic against them. But they both thought it ridiculous and told her to be quiet. Thor realised that he could not do much about the Frost giants and their icy winds, so accepted defeat. All four guests were then lavishly entertained that evening. Even Loki did not get up to any further mischief.

In the morning, Utgard-Loki escorted the group to the castle's entrance and said, "I hope I never see you here again. Before you go, I must explain that I had to use magic against you last night in order to stop you from destroying my castle. You see, Loki could never have beaten Logi who was really wildfire. And how could your peasant's son be faster than Hugi - who was the personification of thought? The drinking horn was connected to the sea, so you could never have emptied it, and the cat was really the world serpent, which you nearly pulled from the sea. And as for struggling with Elli, no one can beat old age."

Thor, Loki and the peasant boy were amazed. The peasant girl blushed. The king repeated his warning.

"Do not return here or I will muddle your heads with more illusions that will leave your heads spinning."

Utgard-Loki vanished and an impenetrable mist began to envelop the castle, whereupon Thor and his band of battlers returned dejectedly to retrieve the goats.

⊕ Osmotherly and Urra

We had yet to complete our crossing the Vale of Mowbray. We left Danby Wiske along Danby Lane and walked across the fields to a cluster of buildings at Oaktree Hill, one of which was a cluttered secondhand car yard.

The rolling hills, criss-crossed with sheep and cattle pastures alongside golden fields of flowering rapeseed, gave the landscape the look of a patchwork quilt. We continued through further fields of crops and over the Northallerton-Teeside railway line. The terrain was flat and occasionally monotonous. My right calf was now sore. Amazing. After successfully negotiating the fells of Lakeland, I thought the rest of the walk would be relatively easy on the legs, so was surprised at my continuing aches and pains. Carol's knee had given her no further problems and she seemed fitter than I was. On we went, over the Wiske River and up past a sad looking terra-cotta brick ruin of the house on Breckon Hill.

At the busy A19 we waited for a long break in the traffic before we crossed. It was impossible to move quickly across the wide road with a full backpack.

Sauntering into the quiet village of Ingleby Arncliffe, we stopped to admire an interesting water tower. The road led on to the crossroads at the village of Ingleby Cross where the Blue Bell Inn beckoned to us. Inside the cosy inn, we ordered coffees and chatted to the manager.

"It's the Bell family who own most of the land around here, including the pub," he enlightened us. It was always interesting to meet folk who were familiar with their local history.

The single other customer added, "The name Ingleby Cross means the settlement of the English at the cross. In the old days, crosses showed the site of the market place, which was called cheaping. This came from the old Anglo-Saxon word *cheap* meaning to buy. Although the Puritans later destroyed the crosses, most of us still call it the cross".

An English couple arrived for a late lunch and we took the opportunity to chat to them as well. The man told us that he had done the Coast to Coast Walk seven years ago. His wife was not a walker but was interested to see two Australians on the walk.

"You flew all the way around the world just to do this walk?" she asked.

"And to visit some dear friends," Carol answered. "We are really enjoying it, especially the lovely B&Bs."

Suitably refreshed, we left the Blue Bell, stopping on the footpath outside the inn to look up at the panorama in front of us. The skyline was dominated by the Cleveland Hills, which were to be our next challenge. There was another road to cross. At the A172 we chatted to Barry and Terry, two walkers who had begun from Robin Hood's Bay and were attempting the distance to St. Bees in ten days. They were using pairs of telescopic staves to accelerate their walking. We had seen a number of walkers use these noisy devices which resembled ski poles. When not in use the staves could be telescoped into a short tube and packed away.

Barry and Terry had started at Claybank Top that morning and were expecting to overnight in Danby Wiske, making it a very full day's walk of twenty-three miles.

We farewelled each other and continued to Arncliffe Wood. This was our first ascent for some days and I continued to walk painfully. Arncliffe Hall, the ancestral home of the Bells, stood solidly on the slope, with the trees of Arncliffe Wood providing a superb backdrop. From here we could see the enormous width of the Vale of Mowbray with its farthest edge disappearing into the hazy distance. Further up the track was a sign to Mount Grace Priory. The Priory had been founded by the Carthusian Order in 1398 and I would like to have seen it, but I was now limping and didn't want to walk further than necessary. Coming to a separation in the track we saw the first signs indicating The Cleveland Way, another well-known walk. Alongside was a smaller sign indicating the path to the village of Osmotherly.

Osmotherly was built around the village cross which was now dedicated to the fallen warriors of previous wars. In the lovely spring weather, groups of people were sipping coffee and chatting out in front of the cafes. There was even an old Morris Traveller automobile, with its original wooden framework, parked in front of the Queen Catherine Inn, our night's stop. Across the road was a general store with the name "Thompson" emblazoned above its entrance. We entered the old shop to buy some toiletries and once inside, I felt as if I had stepped through a time warp. The old fashioned counters, with newspapers carefully stacked beside them, displayed all sorts of produce. Sacks of materials were piled around the interior. It reminded me of the shops that were shown in period films of the early 1900s.

We had arranged to meet Zillah, our Lakeland walking companion, at Osmotherly. Zillah, her son Tim and their dog Doris had finished their walk at Keld. Since they lived a short distance from Osmotherly, Zillah and her husband Frank visited us and spent some pleasant hours chatting and enjoying the ambience of the Queen Catherine.

We selected a cosy nook in the lounge bar and sampled the beverages. We talked about the wonderful country we had walked through, especially along the Swale.

"You probably walked right past our cottage in Gunnerside," Frank said.

Frank and Zillah were renovating a holiday cottage there for retirement. Talk turned to the appreciation of local beverages. I found that I was enjoying cider more than the local brews or wine. The English ciders were light in taste yet satisfying. However, there was one ale that was particularly appealing. Barbara Goodbody's Golden Ale from the Wye Brewery featured an attractive label, depicting a buxom blonde with fluttering eyes. It tasted as good as it looked.

Sir Arthur Bryant, an English commentator and writer had once written of,

"An England of squires, parsons, yeomen and quaint, cider drinking yokels." I had joined the legion of cider drinkers.

* * *

"The path from Beacon Hill onwards is
(thanks to Lyke Wake Walk walkers)
blazed almost wide as a road, and,
with signs at the few points of doubt,
only a genius could go astray."

– A. Wainwright.

Sunday morning and I felt no lingering hangover from last night's cider consumption. We left Osmotherly via the gently ascending quarry road, which brought us back to the Coast to Coast track at Beacon Hill. Again, the morning had begun under full sun, and then gradually disappeared under a thick blanket of clouds. At Beacon Hill we met a young American, Matt from Missouri who, it transpired, was heading towards the same B&B at Urra as we were. So the three of us continued the walk together. At Beacon Hill there was also a marker, which indicated the beginning of the Lyke Wake Walk.

This famous walk crossed hill and dale for forty-two rugged miles to reach its destination at Ravenscar on the coast. For inclusion in the Lyke Wake Walkers Club, one had to cover the distance in twenty-four hours. Male members were called *Dirgers*, while female ones were known as *Witches.* The club was formed in 1955 and since then more than 130,000 people have risen to the challenge of completing the arduous walk. Arthur Puckrin completed the distance in a little over ten hours in 1957. His brother, Phil, trumped him and cut the time in half to five hours in 1971. To add to these records, in 1973, Louis Kulscar was the first person to complete the walk 100 times. After reading the plaque and noting the strenuous entry conditions, I decided not to apply for membership.

The path continued along through Clain Wood. From here we were to follow the Cleveland Way, and did not see many Coast to Coast signs at all. We learnt that Matt had stayed in the same B&B at Cleator that we had declined so were interested to hear his impressions. He told us that when he had arrived in Cleator and seen the accommodation, he had also been disappointed, but decided that it was all part of the experience of the Coast to Coast Walk and so spent the night there.

This happy trio continued along the track talking and laughing. We hadn't noticed that our path had diverged from the official route, and subsequently lost our way.

We arrived at a four way intersection which, on the map, was to the south of the real path. Carol suggested retracing our steps, but Matt and myself were keen to cut across the fields to where we thought the path was. So we did. Luckily enough we encountered a farmer in his tractor who showed us the way. Our cross country trek eventually brought us to a sealed road where it seemed appropriate to have morning tea.

Another walker appeared along the road. He was a volunteer ranger. He and his fellow rangers often walked parts of the track to make sure that the signs and the track itself were in order. He had walked in many parts of the world and had just returned from a walk in South Africa.

We mentioned our unintended deviation from the official route and suggested that a clear sign be erected at the ambiguous junction we had fallen afoul of.

"I think that a map and compass should be sufficient for walkers. You must remember to keep an eye out for the signs," he said. I didn't pursue the point.

After bidding the ranger goodbye, we continued along the road. We followed the track until it emerged at Huthwaite Green, a place distinguished by a pub and a phone box. Being a Sunday, there were lots of day walkers out, enjoying the sunshine. A number of noisy children were adjusting their boots and daypacks

The village of Ingleby Cross

for an outing. Some older walkers sporting military tattoos on their bare chests had just climbed down from the path ahead. Matt stopped here to make some phone calls, so Carol and I continued. He was a lot fitter than either of us, so we knew he would catch us up.

We skirted the woods on Round Hill and after a hefty climb, found ourselves out on the open land of Live Moor. From here, the wild expanses of the moors with their cliff edges, which rose sharply above the wide Vale of Mowbray, were clearly visible. The overcast sky added a sense of sobriety to the brown landscape and my pack felt heavier. The cool air made the walking a little easier. The narrow track was visible intermittently for miles ahead as it rose and fell along the edges of the elevated moorland. During occasional rests, it was satisfying to look back at the long distances we had crossed over the past few days.

We progressed well and were soon at the top of Carlton Moor where the headquarters of the local gliding club stood out, incongruous in these surroundings. The wind sprang up and kept us refreshed. Matt caught us up and passed by.

"We found ourselves on the wild moors..."

"See you at Urra," he said and was soon far ahead.

The track continued over a succession of peaks and valleys. This was tough going. Much of the track was constructed of large granite slabs to prevent erosion. I saluted the souls who had gone to so much effort to position them on this difficult path. Further ahead were Cringle Moor, Cold Moor and finally Hasty Bank. We wound our way through the confusion of the Wain Stones, a large protrusion of rocks, from which we could see the magnificent panorama of the countryside.

To keep me motivated on the numerous gruelling ascents and descents, I imagined myself, at the end of the day, enjoying the comfort of a deeply cushioned couch. Sitting in the couch I was savouring the fact that we had successfully completed the day's challenges.

Finally at Claybank Top, there was a steep path down to the B1257 and from there, another mile to Maltkiln House. We followed the road down towards Urra, but derived no comfort from that, as we knew we would have to retrace our steps up this same road tomorrow morning.

From previous experience, we had found that the added effort to reach accommodation that was off the main track had always rewarded us in the form of an interesting story, wonderful food and good conversation. Maltkiln House did not disappoint.

Our hosts, Wendy and Gerry first showed us our quarters and then invited us into the lounge room for sherry. Matt had beaten us here by thirty minutes and was already enjoying a glass with Ian and Eileen a couple of Australian walkers. Tea, biscuits and sherry for all.

Maltkiln House was sited in the lush, green valley of Bilsdale. Gerry, an avid historian, suggested that the valley was named after William the Conqueror during a hasty return to York from a brutal campaign in the North.

Dinner for us five guests was taken in the dining room. The exposed heavy beams and quaint wallpaper gave a very cosy feeling to the repast. A cold wind was blowing outside.

AD 1014
Canute

Sweyn died in 1014 while the Norse fleet was stationed on the Thames outside London. On a cold day with the waters of the ancient river lapping at the sides of the longships, the Vikings elected his son Canute as his successor. The English Witan of Saxon elders was not prepared to accept yet another Norse ruler so recalled Ethelred from Normandy to resume his position as king of England. Ethelred sent his son Edward instead. Edward arrived and soon proclaimed the standard that all good Englishmen were to follow: "that the king should be sworn allegiance to without treachery, and that every Norse king was an outlaw for evermore."

This improved the English morale considerably so Ethelred returned to England. Ethelred's other son Edmund challenged his father and set about restoring the family's fortunes in the face of the Danish rule. Edward returned to Normandy.

Ethelred "the unwisely counseled" died and Edmund was left to continue his campaign against Canute.

By 1016, Canute seemed invincible. The Norse had control of most of the land and London was again in Danish hands. Edmund fought a heroic battle against Canute at Ashingdon and lost. He fled to the far west, and like Alfred before him, refused to abandon the great struggle. Canute pursued him, knowing that Edmund "Ironside" would always be an *iron* thorn in his *side*. Canute's councilors advised a negotiation to which he agreed. The treaty suggested a peaceful partition of England and the terms were thus: Edmund would keep Wessex, the hereditary English heartland, while Canute took the rest.

Edmund's unexpected death left the whole land under Danish rule yet again. Canute now had effective control over most of England, and had the military backing to prevent any uprisings.

As a first move, Canute needed to clear out the traitors who had been such burdens for his predecessors, especially Ethelred. Eadric and Aelfric along with some others were killed, and as a final humiliating gesture he collected an astounding amount of silver from the English with which he paid off the Viking fleet, sending it back to Denmark. He then set about to create a stable reign of security and peace. Canute the Viking had become a Christian ruler. He knew that, in order to forge England into a nation, he had to repair the bond between the people and the ruler. He understood that because of betrayals and avoidable hardships brought upon them by some of their previous rulers, the people had lost trust and respect for the crown. Canute's personal vision was for a strong, self-reliant nation. He also married Emma, Ethelred's widow to assist him in this.

To begin national reconciliation, he had a church built at Ashingdon and dedicated it to his victory, as well as to the courage of the English who fought there. He renewed the laws to further recognise the equality of the English and Scandinavian inhabitants. Canute attended the coronation of the new Emperor in Rome in 1027.

Canute was now the most renowned ruler in Northern Europe and some of his councilors were becoming increasingly sycophantic. They proclaimed that he was even more powerful than nature. Canute was canny enough to know that this was not so and one day he assembled an entourage at the shoreline. The courtiers and sycophantic administrators were quite curious as to what the great king had in store for them.

"Here I place my throne, in the sand. None of my decrees or power will make the slightest difference to the movements of the world around us," the king informed the assembly.

"See. I cannot even stop the waters from rising," he said, as the tide gently rose and water streamed towards the feet of the courtiers. He let the saltwater flow over his own feet and said, " Nature is more powerful than man, we must remember to humble ourselves.– The entourage retreated from the rising water. Canute had become a wise ruler.

The First Tremor

HAGAL
(elemental disruption)

For sometime after Balder's death, the gods continued to feel chastened and subdued, resulting in a period of reflection. It had finally dawned on them that they had always given Loki the benefit of the doubt and their laxity had brought them to this crisis. They had allowed Loki to involve them in all sorts of imprudent adventures from which, in order to extricate themselves, they were forced to sacrifice their virtues.

Odin remained perturbed. Balder's death and subsequent exile in Hel's realm signalled the beginning of the end. The Fates had definitely confirmed the inevitability of Ragnarok. What would happen after the final battle?

Odin removed his rune inscribed wand from inside his fur vest and read it. The rune that shone strongly just then was Eoh - the yew tree. This rune was linked with death. Odin knew that the yew was an evergreen, suggesting that death was a doorway to rebirth. He still did not understand how transformation could save him, and what was it, exactly?

As men's armies battled each other, the numbers of atrocities and crimes increased, turning the world into a dangerous and desolate place. All the gods realised that the shadow of Doom was advancing.

As the fates had foretold, certain events began to occur. The first snowflake fell. Others began to fall and soon snow fell all over the world. Men began to shiver and the gods' demeanors turned glum. This was the beginning of the terrible Fimbul-winter.

Harsh, biting winds swept down from the north. The frost giants, sensing a good opportunity to wreak havoc, produced more snow and icy winds, causing a thick layer of ice to form around the northern part of the world. Gradually the ice sheet spread southwards.

The deep winter intensified the battles on earth. The snows and the winds continued to blow for six seasons and the struggle for life on earth grew more desperate.

In the depths of the forests, Loki's wife Anguish kept feeding the marrow of murderers' bones to the two wolves Hati and Skoll whose favourite game was to chase the sun and the moon. Because the battles on earth had provided such a large supply of bones and marrow, the two wolves grew enormously in size. Anguish could no longer contain them, so she released the monstrous pair and they rushed forth in search of the sun and the moon.

The wolves chased the celestial bodies and caught them. Opening their ferocious jaws, the wolves quickly devoured the sun and then the moon. This caused a great gap to appear in the skies and the stars began to quiver. The earth trembled at this disastrous celestial readjustment. A giant tremor was felt around the world, and great quakes rent the earth, dislodging rocks from mountain tops and opening up massive chasms.

This first earth tremor broke the bonds that had kept Loki and Fenris imprisoned in the deep chasm. Loki removed his shattered chains and stood up. He took a deep breath, stretched out and exhaled with satisfaction. He then removed the sword from Fenris' jaw, sliced through the wolf's fetter and secured the sword in his belt. Fenris shook off the remains of his fetter as his large body quivered with the joy of once again being unrestrained. He opened his massive jaws and howled. They were free at last. Now for revenge.

⊕ The Lion Inn at Blakey

Day tripper (fashionably dressed): "I don't know how you can live here."
Dalesman: "It's grand living here on the moors."
Day tripper: "It's so boring. You should come to town and see the sights."
Dalesman: "Nay lad, there's no need. They come, they come."

-extract from the Dalesman Magazine

As today's walk was to be an easy nine miles, we took advantage of the comfortable and interesting place that Maltkiln House was. Gerry showed us his pet pig, and what a size she was! We wandered around the gardens in amongst the hens, viewed the pair of ferrets and saw an ancient rock carefully hollowed out, perhaps used in pre-historic religious ceremonies.

But best of all, Gerry showed us a shortcut to rejoin the Coast to Coast path. We didn't have to retrace yesterday's tiresome steps after all. The sun warmed the land.

We followed the track easily up to another "Round Hill" at the top of Urra Moor, the highest of the North York moors. The weather was distinctly hot and muggy, suggesting a gathering storm later in the day. The track continued to Bloworth Crossing where we almost took the wrong fork, but caught ourselves in time by double checking the map and the compass. Here we crossed over onto a disused railway route, the old Rosedale Ironstone Railway and followed the gentle gradient. However, six miles was still six miles and the sun continued to bake us. There were a number of families walking along this track, obviously enjoying the late spring sun.

The time passed languidly as we walked along this crunchy, cinder-covered track and it was easy to slip into a moving daydream. The billowing clouds gently rolled around in the sky.

I suspected that Wainwright had had a deeply intuitive feel for the history of the land and had designed the walk to allow the walker to experience both its visible and hidden facets. We were indeed fortunate to have the opportunity to explore some of the countryside that this master fell walker had traversed.

Then, through a shallow cutting and around a bend, we saw the imposing image of a solitary building silhouetted against the blue sky. At last - the Lion Inn at Blakey.

We heaved up the last gradient to the welcoming bulk of the inn. Perspiring in the afternoon sun, I imagined what it would be like to arrive here in the dead of winter through the snow. The Lion Inn would be a wonderful sight, no doubt.

The inn was one of Yorkshire's oldest, but not highest, as that record remains with the inn on Tan Hill. Around 1553, the Order of Crouched Monks was given a house plot and ten acres of land on which to build a small chapel and

The Lion Inn at Blakey

associated buildings, as they had been unable to find suitable land in York. One of the buildings was used as an inn. Friar inns were common around the country and a good source of income for the various monastic orders.

Here, in the afternoon, holiday makers were luxuriating in the sun and enjoying the changing moods of a lazy spring afternoon. Inside the massively thick walls were a number of cosy bars and drinking nooks. The subdued lighting and murmurs of patrons added to the friendly feel of the inn. Afternoon cups of tea and a lie down for us.

That evening Carol and I enjoyed a hearty meal in the atmospheric 400-year-old inn. Later, upstairs in our room, unable to find the switch to turn down the heat, I left the bedroom window ajar. During the night I was awoken by a jolt. Something had landed on the bed. Turning the bedside light on, I found it was a cat - probably the house cat searching for mice, so I went back to sleep. Then another jolt. It seemed like there wasn't much hunting inside, so the cat had jumped back onto the bed and out through the window. And stay out, mouser.

AD 1035 Normandy: Duke William

Duke Robert the First of Normandy had two nicknames, Robert the Devil and Robert the Magnificent. A descendent of Rolf the Viking, he had strenuously developed the Duchy of Normandy into a highly organised continental state. One day he found himself in a small village in his duchy and his eye was caught by a tanner's daughter, Herleve. The Duke, being a man who usually indulged his wants, took Herleve for himself and she bore him a son who was named William. Since there was no marriage as such, William was nicknamed "the bastard" by his contemporaries. His childhood was spent in the small town of Falaise.

The Duke continued to expand and fortify Normandy against the neighbouring Franks and occasional Viking marauders. This had taken up much of his time and he was now relatively satisfied that his duchy was well defended.

One morning in 1035, Robert the Magnificent woke up, his servants opened the curtains in the bedchamber of his large castle and brought him a mug of cider, a favourite beverage in those parts.

He made love with Herlerve and dressed. Walking across to the large window he looked out upon his domain with pleasure and announced that he was going on a pilgrimage to Jerusalem, the City of Christ. In those days many rulers were drawn to making pilgrimages to Rome and Jerusalem. Edward the Confessor was said to have built the abbey at West Minster because he was unable to fulfill his duty to journey to Jerusalem. Canute and Alfred before him had also been pilgrims to Rome.

The announcement was quite a shock to his courtiers and councillors. How could he just go on pilgrimage now? And who would ensure that Normandy remained safe while he was away?

"Why, Duke William of course," he told the astonished councillors.

After a brief preparation Robert left for the Holy Land. William was only seven years old at the time and was thrust into a world full of danger and intrigue caused by family rivals, vying for control of Normandy.

Robert died while on his return journey from Jerusalem and the Ducal State was thrown into turmoil. William duly inherited Normandy, and assisted by loyal relatives and councillors, managed to thwart a number of attempts on his life. It was a tough childhood and to survive it, his character was necessarily moulded into one of a ruthless survivor and warrior.

William kept favourable contacts with Edward the Confessor who had spent his childhood exiled in Normandy during Canute's reign. In 1051 William visited England as Edward's guest. It was possible that the childless Edward nominated William as his successor during the visit.

William returned to Normandy to deal with a fresh outbreak by rebellious barons who refused to pay him allegiance. In 1054 after subduing the rebellious elements, he became the acknowledged leader of Normandy.

⊕ Towards Egton Bridge

We breakfasted in the atmospheric dining room of the Lion Inn with two other Coast to Coast walkers, Paul and Bob, whom we had first seen at Beacon Hill two days ago. They had been walking at a similar pace to us, but had overnighted elsewhere. Since the four of us were headed for Egton Bridge, we agreed to meet for dinner that evening.

It was an easy start to the day and the air was already warming up. The road led up to Rosedale Head and then past the White Cross known as "Fat Betty" – a stone sculpted to resemble a human figure. My left shin continued to trouble me and I noticed that a swelling had appeared around the middle of it.

The track led us along roadsides and through moors. Then down to The Trough House, an old stone hut used by grouse shooters. We were now on Glaisdale Moor looking at Great Fryup Head which paraded over a landscape rem-

Beggar's Bridge

iniscent of the Lake District. We walked along the gently sloping gradient of Glaisdale Rigg, all the way down to the village of Glaisdale.

It was a true Spring day. The gentle sun warmed the emerging flowers, which provided a colourful contrast to the sombre stone buildings. Insects were buzzing around, people going about their daily chores. The small grassy area surrounding a war memorial, was an ideal place for having a snack. After the brief break, we followed the road as it curved round in a wide sweep, flanked by cottages, cared for by proud owners.

At the bottom of the sweep was Glaisdale Railway Station which had a small teashop attached to it. Carol bought a couple of slices of date and walnut loaf with which to enjoy afternoon tea. Continuing down further we arrived at a large railway bridge. Tucked off to the side was the original Beggar's Bridge and there was a fascinating story associated with it.

A young man of moderate means named Tom Ferris fell in love with Anne Richardson, a wealthy landowner's daughter. He went to ask her father for his daughter's hand in marriage. But the father refused and sent him packing, adding, "Come back when you've made something of yourself and we'll talk again."

Tom decided to act upon this sage advice and prepared to travel and make his fortune. The night before his departure he arranged to meet his love. They lived on opposite sides of the Esk River, which Tom could normally ford. Unfortunately the river was running high that evening and he was unable to cross over to farewell his lovely. A kiss blown from the lips of each of the lovers was the best they could do. He vowed to build a bridge upon his return so that the Esk would never again separate lovers. Tom went on to become a mayor of Hull and of course returned to claim Anne and fulfill his vow. They married in Glaisdale in 1619.

"The Rover returned from a far distant land,
And claimed from the maiden, her long promised hand.
But he built her, ere he won her, the bridge of his vow,
And the lovers of Egton pass over it now."

Anon.

Ahead was the delightful East Arnecliff Wood, which in the late afternoon sun was a carpet of bluebells beneath a canopy of trees. Through the woods, a track of flat, worn stones known as the pannier-way, a centuries old packhorse track, bordered the Esk. We walked on towards the hamlet of Egton Bridge, which even had its own railway station. The name Egton was derived from *Oketun,* a reference to the numbers of oak trees in the neighborhood. The oak was Thor's tree and signified heroism and fragile strength.

Our destination was The Postgate Inn. The inn sign depicted an intriguing picture of a man dressed as a pilgrim. We booked in and enjoyed our customary afternoon tea.

I later found out that the inn was named after Nicholas Postgate, a Catholic priest who had preached for many years in these parts. During the sporadic religious wars when the Protestants were hunting the Catholics in the name of Christ, Nicholas Postgate was arrested and taken to York. There, the 82-year-old priest was tortured and killed outside the walls of that city, earning the name - Martyr of the Moors. The Postgate Inn paid tribute to his life and death. The inn also featured as The Black Dog Inn in the television series, "Heartbeat".

That evening Paul and Bob arrived as planned. They also decided to stay at the Postgate because the owner of their B&B had not arrived. We ordered some fine foods and sat back to enjoy the local ales and ciders. Paul was in property and Bob had just rejoined the workforce. The laughs flowed, along with the beverages.

AD 1035 England: Edward the Confessor

When Canute died in 1035 he left two sons, Harold "Harefoot", by an English mistress and Harthacanute by Queen Emma. England was now a collection of earldoms including the once mighty Wessex, which was now the personal fiefdom of the ambitious Earl Godwine. An ambitious man, Godwine managed to elect Harthacanute to the English throne. Harthcanute reversed many of the progressive changes his father had implemented and was more interested in developments in Denmark, spending little time in England. He had his half brother Edward (by Emma) recalled from Normandy to help him rule England. After Harthacanute's death in 1042, Edward was elected king. He ruled a vastly different land from that of his father, Ethelred.

A new threat emerged from the Viking lands. Edward discovered that his mother, Emma, was plotting with King Magnus of Norway to invade England.

After he recovered from the shock of such a betrayal, he acted decisively and placed Emma under house arrest and confiscated her royal privileges. The English thoroughly approved of this action, as they were horrified with the possibility of yet another Norse king ruling them.

Edward, who had spent his formative years in Normandy, added Norman staff to his administration as well as maintaining his English courtiers. His biggest problem was that of Earl Godwine and his equally ambitious sons. Harold, one of Godwine's sons, had maintained good relations with the House of Wessex and Edward. Old Godwine himself had designs on the monarchy and was waiting for the right opportunity to pounce. He hindered Edward at every opportunity. Godwine had also been implicated in the murder of Edward's brother, young Alfred, some years previously.

It all came to a head when Edward's brother-in-law, Count Eustace, was making a state visit and a fight developed between the Dover townsfolk and Eustace's retainers in which the retainers were killed. Edward ordered Godwine to ravage Dover, the traditional punishment for a town, which caused harm to the king's guests. Godwine refused as Dover was on his lands and raised an army to defy the king.

The Witan was called in to judge the affair and in the end Edward forced Godwine and his family into exile where they found shelter with relatives in Flanders.

This left Edward in sole rule of England. However, the forced departure of the Godwines left a gap in the nation's power structure, which Edward attempted to partially fill with more Norman appointments. In 1051 the king's cousin, Duke

William of Normandy, paid a state visit to England. Although still a teenager William may have been offered the crown privately by Edward, although this was probably a later fabrication by the Norman administration. Edward and his wife were childless so needed to make adequate provision for the succession, and it appeared that Edward thought highly of William.

The other problem was Harald Hardraada of Norway, an opportunist who was always ready to invade any wealthy, unprepared nation. England would soon become a suitable quarry.

In 1030, at the age of fifteen, Harald had been severely wounded in a battle helping King Olaf the Stout to regain his kingdom in Norway. The battle had wiped out Olaf's meagre forces, and Harald managed to escape into the dense forests and found shelter in a small village until his wounds healed. He journeyed to Kiev, the heartland of the Russian Empire. There he came under the guidance of Yaroslav, Lord of Kiev, who taught him the craft of warfare and had him complete his practical education with the Varangian Guard in exotic Constantinople.

This group was the personal bodyguard of the Byzantine Emperor. Harald developed his leadership qualities with this army in varied campaigns in Italy, around Jerusalem, the Holy Land and the Mediterranean. There he gained his nickname Harald Hardraada - *hard man.*

Harald was a single-minded man. His ambition was to wear Norway's crown. In 1045, now thirty and in his prime, Harald left Constantinople and returned to the northern lands. In 1047 King Magnus of Norway died and Harald took the crown. An aggressive person, he spent the best part of the next nineteen years fighting against King Sweyn of Denmark, in a largely futile effort to control Denmark.

⊕ To Littlebeck and The Coast

Today's walk to Grosmont (pronounced Grow Mont), and then to Littlebeck, was only six miles long. This was good because the state of my shin had worsened. During last night's dinner, Bob had told me that the condition was known as "shin splints" and was not unusual amongst walkers.

We followed the private road through the Egton Manor Estate past a toll-house, which displayed the old toll fees for various types of vehicles.

1 Horse 2 wheels	*4 pence*
Motorcar 4 wheels	*1 shilling*
Motor Bus	*3 shillings*
Tractor	*1 shilling*
Hearse	*6 pence*
	Egton Estate Office
	Aug 1948

It was an easy walk to Grosmont, a popular tourist spot. The North Yorkshire Moors Railway passed through the town, greatly adding to its appeal. We planned to take a ride on the steam train. Since we had arrived early, we sat in the cosy dining room, drinking coffees and eating Bakewell Tarts, those lovely English cakes, and waited for the train.

Some years ago, the authorities had closed the railway line as part of the overall rationalisation of services. Luckily, a group of enthusiasts resurrected the line to the cheers of many rail enthusiasts around the country. The railway line and parts of this area were often seen on the television series "Heartbeat".

There was a souvenir shop next door that sold all sorts of "Railwayana" and tourist goods.

Soon enough a steam train chuffed in alongside the platform puffing dense clouds of steam and spraying fine particles of grit. People disembarked, and all of us who had been waiting, boarded the train, ready to enjoy our railway adventure. Two steam whistle hoots sounded and the train slowly pulled out of the station. It was a pleasant journey and I was glad of the chance to rest my legs.

The train stopped at Pickering and then at Goathland for an opportunity to visit the TV village of Aidensfield and the Aidensfield Arms shown in "Heartbeat".

We returned to Grosmont refreshed and ready for the next four-mile hike. It was a continually steep climb up Fairhead Lane, which looked quite magnificent in this exceptional spring weather. Up onto Sleights Moor and then across the A169. We followed the track as it wound down towards Littlebeck; a charming village clustered around the banks of a small stream named Little Beck. The stone buildings, a small church and a collection of holiday townhouses gave it a fairytale look. I looked for a sign to our B&B but couldn't find one.

So where was Intake Farm, our B&B for the night? I asked a youngster who was playing with his brother, if he knew where it was. He pointed up a hill and said, "It's about a mile and a half all the way up that hill."

"Thanks," I said through clenched teeth and groaned. Not having read the map diligently, we had missed the fact that it was another mile or so from Littlebeck.

Fully expecting Littlebeck to be the day's destination, I had already prepared myself to shed my pack and collapse in the heart of this village by the beck. Now I had to gird my loins and carry my pack up another hill. I was sick of walking. Carol wasn't fazed; she took the news in her stride. Crossing the bridge near the church, we found a stone engraved with an arrow and the words *Intake Farm.* We followed the road up the hill. It was becoming quite overcast and cool. Again, the thought that kept me going was that every place that had been sited off the track was worth the extra effort.

Up the hill, under a threatening sky, was a farm, but no sign indicating "Intake Farm" was visible. But this had to be it. We wandered around to the front door and a woman came out to greet us. She was Judith and this was indeed Intake

Farm. It looked very comfortable inside. After we had cleaned up, Judith took us for a tour of the farm while there was still light. She and husband Robert had three lovely daughters and raised cattle and sheep on their farm.

Over a delicious dinner of leek mornay and rhubarb crumble, Judith told us about other walkers, including an athletic female who had done the whole Coast to Coast Walk in eight days!

Afterwards we spent some time reading. *Intake Farm* meant a farm taken in from the moors. I also read in one of the local history pamphlets that Father Nicholas Postgate was arrested near Littlebeck before being taken to York all those years ago.

* * *

We woke to a cold morning. This was to be our final day of walking and my shin was quite inflamed. I listened to Carol's suggestion and arranged for my pack to be transported along with hers to Robin Hood's Bay.

We enjoyed our last English breakfast, ate the boiled eggs with lots of tasty homemade wholemeal bread, a variety of local jams, and finished with hot tea. Outside the weather didn't look good. A few large raindrops flattened themselves against the windowpanes as the wind played havoc with the trees.

We made our way back down to the village and followed the leafy track along Little Beck. Under the cover of the trees, where the wind wasn't able to penetrate easily, the merry chirping of the birds blended with the splashes of the water trickling in the beck producing a medley of forest sounds.

The path diverged from the beck and climbed uphill to an unusual rock formation. The Hermitage was a curiosity, a single chamber hewn out of a solid boulder. It was the work of George Chubb, who completed it in 1790; the year Wordsworth began his European walking tour. Standing inside it, I imagined the amount of effort that had gone into it and wondered what had driven him to do it. Further on we came to Falling Foss, a large waterfall which had pre-announced its presence by the wonderful sound of cascading water. The track continued to a picnic ground and soon veered away from the beck.

Then we climbed up to Sneaton Low Moor. Up here, outside the protection of the woods and the valleys, the wind blew strongly and the sky had darkened, threatening us with storms. It was a marvellous view, the windblown trees starkly silhouetted against the dark, grey sky. The brown sinewy heather lay close to the ground as if to avoid the worst of the wind. There was even a weathered sign to Soulsgrave Farm. It was sad to realise that this was our final walking day on the Coast to Coast journey.

We took our last steps on moorland and crossed over a stile into a ploughed field. The persistent gusts of wind forced us to find a hollowed out ditch where we could have our lunch. Snuggled close to a hedgerow grew a bunch of Lilies of the valley, the flower of Ostara, Norse goddess of Spring and a friend of Freya's. Having eaten our sandwiches we returned to the track by squeezing through a narrow laneway overgrown with nettles and prickly bushes. The wind blew us down the road to Hawkser and remained our blustery companion. We followed the map carefully, as there were no Coast to Coast signs to be seen. There were a number of caravan parks perched on the slopes approaching the cliffs.

Finally, we came upon the North Sea, leaden in colour, brooding. In the distance, whitecaps indicated friction between air and water. The wind was exceptionally strong here, and I wondered why so many English folk chose to holiday in spots like these. Maybe, along with their Norse ancestors, they relished the raw weather along this coast. It was too windy and cold to halt, so we kept walking. The track brought us to the edge of the precipitous cliffs where we simply had to stop to appreciate the panorama.

We had now walked most of the 190 miles across England. Just eighteen days ago we had left St Bees and the Irish Sea behind us, crossed Lakeland, the limestone plateau, the valleys of the Dales and the North Yorkshire Moors, and now almost unbelievably, we were standing at the edge of the cliffs overlooking the North Sea. The weather was starting to look meaner. The few seagulls that were still around seemed to be making off to find shelter. A few splats of rain bounced off our Goretex coats. A squall was coming in from the sea and I could see a curtain of rain move with it. Brrr, that water looked cold. The forlorn sea seemed agitated due to the approaching storm. An image of an open Viking longboat flickered by and disappeared.

AD 1066
England's Crown

In 1052, the exiled Earl Godwine invaded England and Edward was forced to reinstate his family. It was a humiliating action from which Edward never fully recovered. Godwine himself died shortly after and his son Harold distinguished himself as one of England's best generals. Harold provided solid support to Edward as they remained on good terms throughout the recent upheavals precipitated by old Godwine.

Harold made a visit to the continent but was captured by a Norman noble and escorted to Duke William's court in Normandy. Harold was invited to fight for the Duke in a local skirmish and later reluctantly swore an oath upon a chest of holy relics that he would support William's claim to the English throne after Edward's death. This oath was made under some duress, as William was insistent and would likely have imprisoned his guest otherwise. Harold returned to England where he continued to be England's strongman and Edward's military strength.

Early in January of 1066, Edward the Confessor died leaving the issue of succession open to interpretation. Harold immediately claimed the throne. There was no alternative at the time as the only natural heir to the throne was young prince Edgar, inexperienced and certainly no match for the predators likely to be prowling along the English coast. News of Edward's death quickly spread across the seas.

Soon after, a great and marvellous fire was seen in the sky across Europe. In England there was no doubt that it was sent from the heavens to kindle a sacred fire to help the troubled country. Astute readers of the Anglo-Saxon Chronicle may have recognized this heavenly fire as similar to the one seen in 793 which had heralded an earlier change in the island's fortunes - the Viking raids.

With the news of Edward's death, Harald Hardraada of Norway made plans to invade wealthy England. He launched his invasion fleet. There was a favourable north wind, which carried his fleet across the cold North Sea towards the rich and fertile land of England.

Harold Godwinesson had the English crown. The problem was that he had no real military support from the other earldoms to help him keep it. He could not even rely on his brother Tosti to aid him. Tosti had been forced out of Northumbria because of his destructive rule. Harold had not supported his restoration, so Tosti now regarded him as an enemy and was prepared to go to any lengths to regain his territory.

Harold made some astute political moves that positioned him more securely. He knew that sooner or later, William - Duke of Normandy, whom he had sworn allegiance to under duress, would cross the channel to claim *his* right to England's crown, so had stationed an army on the southern coast to prevent this.

William had, in fact, begun assembling an invasion fleet of seven hundred vessels as soon as he had heard of Edward's death. The fleet was now poised to sail. This was no perfunctory fleet; the Duke meant business.

William's crossing was delayed by some weeks due to the disadvantageous north wind, the same one that was carrying the Vikings across the North Sea. In England, Harold could not contain his men any longer. They began returning to their hometowns, as the provisions had run out and the harvest season was on. A small army remained, but there was still no sight of the Norman fleet.

Harald Hardraada's fleet crossed the North Sea and sailed into the wide estuary of the Humber. The fleet of two hundred ships continued up the Ouse towards the old town of Jorvik now known as York. Harold's brother Tosti had switched sides and had allied himself with the Vikings. The Vikings moored near Ricall and began ravaging the countryside. A local army of Northumbrians engaged the Vikings at a place called Gate Fulford, but this only resulted in high casualties for both sides. The Vikings soon captured York. Harald Hardraada moved his troops further inland to Stamford Bridge and camped in the valley, glad of some rest.

Harold Godwinesson received reports of the battle at Gate Fulford and moved swiftly to stem any further invasion of Northumbria. A series of forced marches brought his men to Stamford Bridge.

The Vikings were caught unprepared. Over at the English army's camp, Harold's standard, "The Fighting Man" was moving in the breeze. Surprised by the arrival of the English, Hardraada raised his standard, "The Land Ravager" and caught his breath. Only the swollen Derwent River separated the two armies.

Two armoured and helmeted English soldiers bearing a message for Hardraada and Tosti, crossed the bridge at Stamford and rode across to the Norse camp.

"I am here to tell you the following," the smaller of the English soldiers related to Tosti, "If your army surrenders now, you will be given rule over Northumbria."

In response Tosti asked, "And what is the share of the spoils for my good lord, the King of Norway?"

"For him, seven feet of good English soil!" replied the soldier.

As the two English soldiers returned to their camp Harald Hardraada said to Tosti, "The small one is insolent, yet rides like a king."

"Yes, he is my brother, Harold."

The battle was on. The bridge across the Derwent was the only land gate by which the two armies could encounter each other at close quarters. A large Viking had taken his stand in the centre of it. He stood there, all seven feet of solid Norse muscle, swinging a mighty war axe preventing any engagement at close quarters. Quietly, two English soldiers grabbed a boat from upstream and steered it to position themselves under the wooden bridge. Once they were directly beneath the Viking, a mighty upthrust of a long sword from one of the soldiers removed the Norwegian obstacle. This allowed the English to forge their way across the bridge. The fighting was fierce. At one point Hardraada became furious and rode straight at the English army. His horse stumbled and he was thrown clear. He stood up with a dreadful war axe and charged ahead, leading his men.

Then suddenly, an arrow struck him in the throat; he fell and died. This took the wind out of the Viking army and the English soon routed their enemies. Harold Godwinesson allowed the defeated to return to their ships and depart. Out of two hundred fighting ships, about twenty boatloads of men returned to their lands in Norway.

⊕ Robin Hood's Bay!

According to the map, we had another three miles of coastal walking before reaching Robin Hood's Bay. The ferocity of the wind and the intermittent showers encouraged us to move on. The damned wind, would it never ease? We would have had our fill of seaviews by the time we reached our destination. The walk seemed to take forever but as we rounded Ness Point, for a brief moment, the clouds parted and the sun shone through. Across the inlet the picturesque village of Robin Hood's Bay, precariously perched on the cliffs, was bathed in golden sunlight.

The clouds closed again. There was a wonderful smell of salt spray mixed with fresh rain falling on receptive earth. There was a sense of electricity moving through the cloying air as we made haste towards the little seaside village. The relentless wind had reddened our faces. The rain eased and then stopped.

A solid concrete seawall, designed to prevent further erosion from the battering waves, separated the sea from the village. We hurried through the outskirts of town, passing buildings of Victorian vintage, and found the old main street, which led into the heart of this old smugglers' stronghold.

The steep, narrow road passed by quaint buildings, economically squeezed together to make best use of the limited space. We soon found our B&B with our packs deposited at the front door. Carol knocked, but there was no response. I tried knocking, but the place was deserted. It began to rain again so we picked up our packs, determined to find alternative shelter. At the bottom of the laneway was a small general store, which also provided B&B facilities. Yes we were interested.

We struggled with our packs up the narrow winding staircase to our room and sat down, very glad to be out of the weather. Outside, the sound of falling rain increased.

We enjoyed a pot of tea with some of the fruitcake left over from lunch. With the rain pelting down outside, the savvy traveller finds other things to do. There was a lot of reading material to look at, including a history of the town.

Robin Hood's Bay, also known as Bay Town, or simply as The Bay, was settled by the Vikings. Later, due to its convenient position near the sea, smuggling became the main industry. The deceptively tiny houses were built closely together, linked by secret passages. It was popularly quoted that a barrel of goods could be slipped in at one end of town and finish up at the other end, without once seeing daylight. Rudyard Kipling had penned a poem about Bay Town,

Five and twenty ponies,
Trotting through the dark.
Brandy for the Parson,
'Baccy for the Clerk.
Them that asks no questions, isn't told a lie.
Watch the wall my darling,
While the gentlemen go by!

The origin of the name *Robin Hood's Bay* is not known, but probably honours the memory of one of England's most famous folk heroes.

Feeling greatly revived by the afternoon tea, we were keen to explore the town. As the rain lessened we donned our wet weather gear and strode out onto the narrow street. The road was wet and puddles of water had formed between the cobblestones. The smell of newly fallen rain and salt spray was invigorating. The first priority was to dip our toes into the North Sea. We walked down to the stone ramp, which ended at the seafront, and wet our boots in the seawater. By performing this ritual we had completed a walk from one side of England to the other, and as Wainwright may have said, "Well done!"

Next door was the Bay Hotel for the obligatory drink at the Coast to Coast bar. We found the bar and walked in. Perched right on the water, the room had views of the bay and comfortable seats. The photos of scenes from the walk confirmed its association with this marvellous journey.

"A sherry and cider please". Wainwright, in his guidebook, was adamant that he would not be shouting a round of celebratory drinks, "Pay for your own," he wrote. "I'm skint".

There was a visitors' book in which we carefully looked for any recognisable names. Yes, John and Robyn, Ian and Eileen, had all signed the book two days ago. Most of the other entries showed walkers having completed the distance in twelve to thirteen days, which confirmed the average time suggested by the walkers we had met in the pub at St Bees. However, we found that even walking at our pace over the eighteen days, we had hurried. Taking twenty one days to complete the journey would have given us more time to enjoy Grasmere, Kirkby Stephen and Richmond.

The instability of the weather prompted us to continue our exploration of the town without further ado. The reality of reaching our destination had finally sunk in. We had actually crossed from one side of England to the other, on foot! It felt fantastic to have arrived at Robin Hood's Bay. Encouraged by this sense of euphoria we continued our sight-seeing.

The town was a maze of interconnected alleys and laneways ending up in unexpected spots or dead ends. There was an old church, a stone police station and a number of tourist shops which flanked the main street. A small real estate shop advertised some local cottages for rent. One was named Yggdrasil, after the mythological Norse World Tree. Further back from the sea the town opened out a little to accommodate extra dwellings, but viewed from up here, Bay Town seemed to have miraculously shrunk in size, with only a tight clutch of roofs visible to the observer.

It was getting on and time for dinner. The Dolphin Hotel had been recommended for the best food in town. It was a tight squeeze in the bar, but enjoyable. We shared dinner with another couple from our B&B who had arrived there soon after we had. Inevitably we talked about our respective walks. They were midway through the Cleveland Walk and like us, marvelled at the quaintness of this village. The ambience in the bar was warm and cosy, in complete contrast to the cold and bleak weather outside. The sky had grown darker and the rain resumed its showers. The wind, which had never quit, now increased its assault. I peered out through the pub windows and saw that all the shop doors had been secured against the weather. Ordering a round of pints, I asked the barman if this was typical weather and he replied, "It's not usually this rough. Seems like it'll be a corker tonight."

We drank familiar ciders and full-bodied ales, and chatted to the others in the lively bar. Even though it was noisy inside, the increasing din outside, caused by the falling rain and howling wind, was noticeable. What magnificent sounds, especially when we were warm and dry inside. I wondered how athletic types who attempt to walk the Coast to Coast in only eight days would cope with this rough weather.

An old salt came over and joined our table. He introduced himself.

"They call me Rick. My family settled in these parts a long time ago."

He seemed thirsty and maybe if we wet his whistle we might even get to hear an interesting story. It was just a pint he required, thanks, and continued.

"Yes, the old Vikings settled here and made a living from the sea. Even the area around here is called *Fygling* an old Scandinavian word which means "taking sea birds.'"

"What about the stories of the smugglers?" we asked.

"Because the Bay is so close to the water, it was always perfect for smuggling goods. In those days, the tax on goods was so high that people could afford very little. So smugglers filled in the gaps."

We all emptied our pints and refilled. "Ah, the old days," Rick sighed and cleared his throat.

"You know that many times, the authorities would mount raids on the Bay, but we knew how to move the goods well before they arrived," he said.

"The folk here always helped out each other in times of trouble. When that ship was wrecked at Whitby last century, our lads wheeled lifeboats across the snow to help save the shipwrecked souls. And storms. We have had some rippers.

About two hundred years ago, there was such a big storm and heavy seas that part of the town was washed into the sea. The place looked a lot different the next day. You can see the difference in some of the old drawings."

Suddenly an almighty crack and boom shattered the noise of the bar and the lights dimmed.

"What the hell was that?"

"Sounds like a big storm is about to hit us," said Rick. "Best get back to

Robin Hood's Bay

your lodgings before the heavens empty the big bucket upon us all."

We took his advice. The rain had eased off, so the four of us bade him good night and made our way out into the cold night. The wind howled and a heavy salt spray permeated the air. Anything that wasn't nailed or bolted down firmly, was being scraped along or flapped around by the wind. The reflection of the streetlights sparkled from the black, wet and worn road stones. All the doors and shutters had been secured leaving little slats of light visible through the cracks.

We walked briskly through the deserted village along the narrow road and soon arrived back at our B&B. Saying goodnight to our dinner companions, we climbed up to our cosy room. Time to hit the sack and enjoy the elements from

"We had completed a walk from one side of England to the other..."

the comfort of our lodgings. I hoped that the buildings in Bay Town could withstand the storm, and that it would be over by morning. The violence of the weather increased. The chaos outside sounded like battling armies.

AD 1066
The Battle at Senlac Hill

After destroying Hardraada's Viking army, Harold was allowed no rest. Down in the south, the north wind, which had kept the Norman fleet stationed on the coast of Normandy had now become a south wind. This allowed the large fleet to cross the channel and the Normans landed at Pevensey on the English coast. William's army was soon in control of the surrounding area. The news of the Norman invasion reached Harold in York, and once again he had to force march his men to engage with an invading` army. Harold marched via London to collect more fighting men and then continued southwards. The experienced soldiers were armed with axes, swords and spears, but the new recruits, the majority being farmers and peasants, had clubs and pitchforks for weapons.

Harold and the fleetest of his army arrived breathlessly near Hastings and set up a battle command, waiting for the rest of his men to arrive. He ordered his two standards to be set up above the English camp on Senlac Hill near the Hoary Apple Tree. *The Golden Dragon* was the ancient ensign of Wessex and *The Fighting Man* was Harold's personal device signifying that Anglo Saxon kings fought on foot alongside their men.

It was Saturday morning, the feast of Saint Calixtus. The Norman leaders, strongly allied with the Church, partook of Holy Communion on such days. William also did.

He then spoke to his men and reminded them of their mission, of their duty to him and to Normandy on this foreign soil. He told them of the fame of the Normans in war and reminded them of the pledge that the English king, Edward, had given him. William assured them that he was the rightful heir to the

English throne.

He spoke angrily about the English reputation for cruelty, the terrible massacres of St Brice's Day. Of how the English could not shake off the Viking attacks and how they had tortured and slain his own cousin Alfred.

The massive Norman army was primed and ready to battle the English. The army was made up of three sections. First were the Bretons, led by Alan Rufus of Brittany. Then a large group of adventurers from France and finally the Normans themselves. The army marched from Hastings to Telham Hill from where they saw the English camp identified by their two standards.

William attacked.

The English soldiers stood together, forming a wall of human flesh protected by a veneer of shields. Each man stood shoulder to shoulder with his fellow soldier presenting an impenetrable boundary on Senlac Hill. Both sides of the hill were protected by large boggy marshes, forcing the Normans to advance straight-ahead.

The Norman archers began to bombard the English with volleys of sharp arrows. The wall of Englishmen remained firmly in place. Volley after volley of sharp arrows failed to breach it, and the Normans finally ran out of the lethal projectiles. William ordered his foot soldiers to advance, which they did, yelling, "God help us." Harold's men countered with, "God Almighty" and "Holy Cross." The English hurled their javelins and began to repel the Normans. Then the cavalry was sent forward, but they could not break through. A shout broke out and it seemed that the Duke had been felled. It was true; his horse had toppled, bringing him down. A wave of insecurity spread amongst the Norman soldiers and they began losing ground. The Duke found his legs, mounted another horse and yelled, "William is alive! Fight! Fight!"

He pushed forward and his men rallied around. William rode and cut his way towards the hill which Harold and his men were holding. The Normans had regained their spirit, and now had to breach the English wall. The English stood firm, as if rooted in the soil. William then turned to tactics. He tried to tempt the English out of their unassailable position by ordering some of his men to pretend to flee. The English, seeing a chance to press their advantage, followed. They began to chase the Normans, but now found themselves surrounded by the enemy and were cut down. Late in the afternoon, the Normans managed to acquire more arrows and proceeded to inflict further damage on the English. During one of these terrible volleys, Harold was struck down, apparently by an arrow through his eye. With the felling of Harold, the tide of battle finally turned in the Normans' favour. However, Harold's loyal men kept battling till the end.

By sunset, the English hill had been taken and this southern part of England was William's.

Ragnarok

GER
(The harvest
of past deeds)

The tremors that had freed Loki and Fenris continued to shake the world. Mountains that had been perpetually covered by ice and snow began to tremble and collapse. Large cracks appeared in the earth allowing noise and light to penetrate the secluded recesses where the dwarves lived. Some of the dwarves came out of the ground to investigate while others burrowed deeper, seeking shelter. The large Serpent, which had lain peacefully wrapped around the earth, awoke. Perplexed at all the commotion, it rose to the surface of the sea and crawled out onto the land, causing tidal waves.

The time decreed by the fates was fast approaching. Loki and Fenris made their way to the edge of the foam-flecked ocean, from where they could see the Plain of Vigrid, the foretold arena of the final battle. Tidal waves had dislodged and set afloat the Ship of the Dead, a disgusting looking vessel made from bones, corpses and fingernail pairings. It was an ungainly hulk but seemed to float on the water, so the two creatures of chaos clambered aboard and steered it towards Vigrid. From behind another fog-enshrouded promontory, a second boat appeared, filled with frost giants who bristled with ugly weapons and a hatred of the gods. They hungered for revenge against the beings that had never shared the world's blessings with them.

From his vantage point on Bifrost, Heimdall saw the gathering hordes and sounded his horn to warn the gods of the approaching final battle. It was said that the final call to arms was heard around the world. The gods had been preparing for this hour since the onset of the terrible Fimbul winter. Setting out on their steeds and chariots, they blazed across the sky towards the Plain of Vigrid. The Valkyries woke the slain warriors from their nightly slumber in Valholl and escorted them to Vigrid where they joined their gods in readiness for the final battle.

Surt the fire giant appeared with his sons, creating fiery flashes in the sky. They stormed Bifrost, intending to destroy Asgard, but the bridge crashed beneath their weight and they fell earthwards to the battlefield.

The Ship of the Dead and the vessel of frost giants reached the shores of Vigrid, where the occupants noisily clambered over the sides of the boats and stood on the shore. Hel, the goddess of the underworld, joined the throng of giants and outcasts. Loki led the dishevelled masses with their torn and rotting clothes towards the battleground. The Serpent crawled along after them. All the combatants had arrived on the plain.

The gods were at a disadvantage. Odin had only one eye, Tew one hand, and Frey, who had used his sword to silence Fenris' terrible howls, had no weapon but a stag's horn. Thor still had his mighty hammer and he was making thunder. The other gods were not as well suited to warfare, but stood resolutely in the face of impending disaster.

Mounted upon his eight-legged steed, Sleipnir, Odin surveyed the arena in front of him. He had asked himself repeatedly, how would transformation help him in these last moments? As he patted his steed, he noticed a magnificent white moonflower growing nearby. Dismounting to pick the large white flower, his rune wand slipped out from inside his fur vest and fell onto the ground. The rune wand was glowing and every rune inscribed on it was illuminated as if vying for his attention.

He picked it up and held it in his left hand. He closed his eye and let his right index finger be drawn to one of the runes. He opened his eye and saw that his finger had overlapped two of them, Eoh and Beorc. Eoh had already resonated with Odin previously and he knew it dealt with death and rebirth while Beorc was the rune of purification, renewal, healing and recovery.

Odin bent down to pick the white flower, which he knew was Beorc's flower. He placed the flower and the rune wand inside his vest and remounted Sleipnir. The chieftain of the gods galloped back to join his fellow gods.

Their opponents moved around, some belching fire and smoke, others creating eerie noises. Birds of prey were seen in the sky, because there would be a lot of carrion left for them at the end of this day.

It was as if a signal had been given; the two sides let loose at each other. All the hatred and ill will that had been festering now broke loose and was hurled into the maelstrom. The Valkyries and their chosen warriors fought valiantly against the masses of frost giants who used sharp icicles and huge blocks of ice as weapons.

The combat was face to face. Fenris, remembering Odin's treachery, went at him. Odin faced the slavering jaws. His wand of runes was of no use to him now. It seemed that Odin, who was privy to many secrets, was ultimately powerless against this creature of chaos. Was all his questing for knowledge and wisdom going to end like this, crunched between the jaws of a wolf? Fenris opened his jaws and consumed Odin in one piece. Frey who was fighting Surt, saw Odin's predicament and momentarily turned around to help, managing to strike the wolf a fatal blow. The giant took this advantage to cut Frey down with his flaming sword.

Loki and Heimdall searched each other out. They were destined to fight to the end. Loki still smarted from Heimdall preventing him taking Freya's necklace. Heimdall knew that Loki was a cunning opponent, but he relished using his extraordinary senses to beat him. Their battle was short, intense and painful, but in the end each destroyed the other.

The one-handed Tew was fatally bitten by the dog from Hel-gate, who in turn, suffered a tremendous and deadly gash to his underbelly. Thor searched out his old rival, the Serpent. Amongst the noise, fire and screams, he faced the creature and lifted his hammer high above its head, bringing the hammer down onto its scaly skull. The Serpent shrieked with pain and began to convulse, throwing Thor off balance. However, after taking nine steps back to recover his balance, he was drowned by the poison that spilled from the dying Serpent. The frost giants and the warriors fought till none were left.

Every one of the gods and goddesses who had fought at Vigrid had perished. Loki and Fenris had been destroyed. The hordes of evil-smelling dead and the vengeful giants had been annihilated in the maelstrom that swept the Plain of Vigrid.

There would be no new stories of the gods' heroic deeds or of the cunning machinations of Loki or the frost giants. All of them were gone, all except Surt, the fire giant. He was still alive and he stood there on the charred battleground, pleased with the destruction he saw around him. His flaming sword was still in good order and he was uninjured. He began searching the battlefield for his sons. He found them slumped on the ground, dead. They had fallen from the broken Rainbow Bridge, and never recovered. Having nothing left to live for, in a final fit of rage he hurled a great ball of fire at Yggdrasil, cursing the gods for the death of his sons. The fire consumed its branches and devoured the palaces of the gods. A great conflagration now overtook the world. Flames consumed the cities of men. The noble forests burned as creatures fled unsuccessfully from the fatal fire. The waters in the lakes boiled, killing the fish. Monstrous clouds of smoke rose into the atmosphere, choking the birds of the sky.

Eventually the fire subsided and the world was left scorched. As the great globe of the earth smouldered beneath a layer of ashes, a gurgling sound was heard. Presently a great tide of water moved across the world, engulfing even Surt who had exhausted himself in his frenzy. The earth began to cool and soon froze.

After some time the warmth of the sun began to melt the ice and snow revealing that all life had not perished in the final battle. Beneath the roots of the scorched Yggdrasil a man and a woman cautiously emerged from their haven to look at this new world. They would eventually repopulate the world.

AD 1066
A fiery Crown!

William had won the battle at Senlac Hill, but this was no conclusive invasion. Only area by area did the English begin to accept him as their new ruler. The people of London would not surrender to these upstart Normans. Dysentery was the next foe the Normans had to deal with. This took a toll on the troops and the conqueror himself was laid up for a month. Recovering from this setback, the Normans then approached the south bank of London, torched Southwark and completed a long circle around London's environs. All of this in winter, with the deep snows and difficulties of finding enough food for the army. As the army gradually approached London again, the spirit of the resolute town's inhabitants faltered and they surrendered.

England badly needed a king and in the absence of any other suitor, William was grudgingly accepted.

On Christmas day 1066 a great crowd gathered in and around Westminster Abbey to witness his coronation. The archbishops, Aldred of York and Geoffrey of Coutances, presented him to the combined congregations in English and French respectively.

However, the loud shouts and yells of acceptance and congratulations so alarmed the Norman soldiers guarding the abbey area, that they assumed that a rebellion was underway and so began torching the surrounding buildings. This was an old Norman tactic to isolate and subdue rebellious upstarts.

The congregation, seeing the encroaching flames and smelling acrid smoke, fled in terror whilst the agitated king-to-be was left with only the clergy to complete the tradition of pouring the holy oil to anoint the monarch's forehead.

Was this coronation by fire, the auspicious beginning for William the First's reign over England, the same fire alluded to by the marvellous comet in the sky earlier that year?

* * *

Epilogue

Spring time

After the terrible events of Ragnarok and the destruction of the old gods, the people expected a new period of enlightened rule to eventuate, one that would put an end to all the bloodshed and turmoil so recently experienced. Odin, Thor and the old gods had perished in the final battle. Only Balder the god of light, was expected to return.

Unsown fields
Will wax with fruit
All ills grow better,
Balder will return.

Christianity had also brought with it the promise of salvation in the Easter miracle of resurrection.

As winter's icy hold over the land eased, Eostre the goddess of Spring appeared, manifesting in the melting snows and lengthening days. The forests discarded their mantles of heavy snow assisted by gusts from the fresh spring winds. Creatures awakened from their annual hibernation and again appeared on the surface of the land, foraging for food. The sun emerged to once more broadcast its munificence across the land. Balder had returned.

However, as the Normans continued consolidating their power by force, the people could have been forgiven if they thought that the struggles encountered during Ragnarok had also returned. There was much hatred and resistance against these brutal self-appointed guardians of the English crown.

The Normans desperately needed to prove their divine right to rule the Anglo-Saxons. They claimed legitimate rule from the descendants of the early Britons who had crossed the channel to exile in Gaul during the Anglo-Saxon invasions. The Normans reinforced the stories of Edward's promise of the crown to

William, and of Harold's betrayal of his oath of allegiance. The invaders from Normandy would definitively reshape the Engla-Lande of the Anglo-Saxons in the years to come.

The last of the line of Saxon kings, Prince Edgar, died 59 years later in 1125, and so came to an end Cerdic's ancient House of Wessex, originally descended from Odin and Adam.

A strange tale

There is a strange tale told in the Golden Valley in Herefordshire near the Welsh border. Harold Godwinesson knew this area well from the earlier times he had spent fighting here.

The tale insists that Harold did not die on Senlac Hill. The last great stand against the Normans was made at sunset and with darkness descending on the chaos, some fled to safety and many others died. Examination and identification of bodies could not be confirmed in the dark.

Harold's first wife, Edith Swans-neck had been waiting with some monks from Waltham Abbey (which Harold had helped to found), and under cover of dark they searched for his body. It took some time as they had to move about quietly, but they did find it, surrounded by the bodies of his men. Harold was gravely injured and unconscious, but still alive. They removed all evidence of his royal ranking and transferred them to a corpse close by. Then they spirited him away to safety.

The following day, Edith was required to identify the body of her king, which she did. Thus was confirmed the death of Harold Godwinesson. William the Conqueror ordered the body of the defeated king to be demeaningly buried on the shore to, "Guard England against invasion".

Eventually, Edith and the monks moved the real Harold to the seclusion of the Welsh borderland where he could convalesce in safety. Harold gradually recovered, but his bout with death had changed him forever. He became a hermit in the Golden Valley. Stories were heard of a holy man living in those parts who had a great scar across his empty eye socket reminiscent of Odin, the old pagan Allfather.

⊕

In the morning, the sun shone over a moist Robin Hood's Bay, with its wet, glistening stone streets. The air smelt so fresh and clean. Last night's storms had passed, leaving only a memory of armies battling. It had been a tremendous walking journey, through time as well as space. We packed our bags and carried them out to the waiting taxi. On the stone wall across the street, a large raven was standing and looking at me. As I returned his stare, the raven gave a loud caw, almost like a laugh. He too had survived the storm.

⊕

Appendix

Adventure Beckons! - Practicalities

If you too have been inspired to follow in the footsteps of the Romans, Anglo-Saxons and Vikings on a wonderful adventure, the following pages will answer some of those questions about the doing of it.

Timing:

The thing about travel is that any time is the right time. It's just that you will have different experiences.

We began our walk in late April, which is mid-late spring in England. The most popular time is summer, from June to August. However during summer, the numbers of walkers can add accommodation problems adding further challenges to the walk.

Starting from St Bees:

From Australia we flew to London and travelled to Carlisle in the north of England. From Carlisle, there are frequent trains, which stop at St Bees.

Returning from Robin Hood's Bay:

Catch a taxi to Scarborough, bus to York and train to London. Alternatively, one of the companies that provide walkers' support services can arrange transport back to St Bees.

Distances:

We averaged around 17km a day. That's about 3-4km per hour. Your body will let you know the distances suitable for it. Don't overdo it, especially the first 3 days of your journey. If you think you will need more time for your walk, you need to plan for it. We took 18 days whereas others have taken as little as 8 days. We found that even 18 days did not provide us with enough time to fully appreciate the views and visual feasts, which were presented to us.

What to take:

Light as possible is better than little as possible. A well-fitted backpack and a small day pack for touring city sights. Walking shorts and/or travel trousers; 2-3 cotton shirts or T-shirts; 3 sets of underwear; a fleece jacket; Gore-Tex raingear; pyjamas or equivalent; light shoes for the evenings; a staff; sunhat and sunglasses; medical kit; aluminium water bottle; camera; diary; guide books; maps and compass; toiletries; laundry liquid.

Feet:

We found firm-soled boots better than the flexible type ones because of the uneven rocky paths. Wear your boots for some weeks to make sure they're suitable. Wear two pairs of socks: a thin inner sock to wick moisture way and a thickly cushioned outer sock.

Laundry:

Handwash the day's undies, socks and shirt every night. Travel stores stock a concentrated liquid laundry soap that makes the job easier. Most of the laundry will dry during the night in the heated rooms. Some B&Bs can provide washing facilities if you ask nicely.

Water:

This is the stuff that keeps you alive. Drink as much as possible. We occasionally ran out of water, but fresh water was easily available at the villages.

Will you get lost?

The signposting along some of the route is good. But you need to be constantly aware of where you are in reference to the map. The guidebooks have detailed maps, and you can also need to get specific maps of the path's entire length. (See Maps and Compass).

Guide books:

We travelled with Wainwright's 'A coast to Coast walk.' It has detailed maps and directions for the entire walk. It may require some updating as conditions change occasionally. Paul Hannon's guide was a newer version. Also used was Ronald Turnbull's 'Coast to Coast' guidebook. There is a lot of information available on the Internet. Search under "Coast to Coast".

Maps and Compass:

It is mandatory to take a compass and the correct detailed maps, as it is possible to lose your way depending on weather conditions.

We used the "Strip Maps" published by Michael Joseph. These are the O/S; Ordinance Survey maps listed as Outdoor leisure 33 and 34. They cover the entire route showing detailed areas about 2 miles either side of the track. Having the compass enabled us to double-check our direction, and saved us from getting lost a number of times.

Food:

There are a good variety of foods available all around. In the B&Bs were ate a full English breakfast and ordered a packed lunch, as it can be difficult to buy food on much of the route. In the evenings, some of the B&Bs can provide dinner, or the inns have a good selection to choose from.

First Aid:

Bandage, Band-Aids, sunscreen 15+, Swiss army knife (with corkscrew), aspirin, antiseptic cream and Betadine for cuts.

Animals:

Lots of sheep, cattle and occasionally dogs. When walking through fields it makes sense not to disturb the animals if possible.

Shelter:

B&Bs, hotels, Youth Hostels, caravan parks and camping grounds are available. Some walkers even ask permission from farmers to camp on their land or sleep in the barns. There is a small charge for this.

Walking as preparation:

Before attempting a walking journey of this length, it's important that you prepare your body by doing some weekend walks of 2 or more hours length. Start 4 to 6 weeks before you begin the big walk. This will give you time to adjust muscles, feet and boots.

Reading as preparation:

Reading about the history and other walkers' experiences on the route will give you a greater appreciation for your own journey and prepares you somewhat for your challenges.

Money:

Travellers cheques or credit cards are readily accepted. Having two days cash on hand makes it easier.

York:

The ancient capitol of Yorkshire is certainly worth a few days visit. There are a number of interesting city tours including one of York Minster.

Some one to carry your pack?

There are a number of companies that will arrange to carry your pack from one village to the next, leaving you with the pleasure of only carrying a day pack. Search on the internet under "Coast to Coast" for the most suitable. These companies can also arrange to book your accommodation for a fee. They also provide guided tours.

Recommended Reading

A Short History of the English People	John Richard Green Macmillan & Co 1907
Credo	Melvyn Bragg Hodder & Stoughton 1996
In Search of the Dark Ages	Michael Wood Penguin, BBC Books 1994
The Story of English	McCrum, Cran, Macneil Faber & Faber 1986
History of England	George Macaulay Trevelyan Longmans 1929
The Conquest of England	Eric Linklater Hodder & Stoughton 1966
Life in Anglo-Saxon England	R.I. Page BT Batsford 1970
The Saxon Kings	Richard Humble Weidenfeld & Nicolson 1980
Harold, The last Anglo Saxon King	Ian W. Walker Sutton Publishing 1997
Vikings!	Magnus Magnusson Bodley Head & BBC 1980
The Vikings, Lords of the Sea	Yves Cohat Thames & Hudson 1992
The Vikings	Jonathan Wooding Landsdowne Publishing 1997
When Longships Sailed	Editors of Time-Life Time-Life USA 1998

The Normans	R. Allen Brown Boydell Press 1984
William the Conqueror	David C Douglas Eyre & Spottiswoode 1966
The Lost Gods of England	Brian Branston Thames & Hudson 1974
Discovering Place Names	John Field Shire Publications 1971
The Coast to Coast Walk	A.J. Wainwright Michael Joseph 1995
Walking in England	Lonely Planet Publications 1997
Coast to Coast Walk	Paul Hannon Hillside Publications 1999
Coast to Coast	Ronald Turnbull Dalesman 1998
Wordsworth and his world	F E. Halliday Thames & Hudson 1970
Myths of the Norsemen	H.A. Guerber George Harrap & Company
Larousse Encyclopedia Of Mythology	Edited by Felix Guirand Paul Hamlyn 1964
World Mythology	Donna Rosenburg Harrap 1986
Runes	David V Barrett Hodder & Stoughton 1995
Signs & Symbols	Miranda Bruce-Mitford Dorling Kindersley 1996

* * *

DATES

BC

55	Julius Caesar invades Britain

AD

43	Claudius sends army of occupation to Britain.
121	Hadrian builds wall against the Picts
306	Constantine declared emperor
402	Beginning of Roman withdrawal
410	Rome is sacked
436	Adventus Saxonum
519	The Founding of the kingdom of Wessex
597	Abbot Augustine arrives in Kent
640	Bega arrives in Cumbria
793	Danes ravage Lindisfarne
800	Egbert becomes king of Wessex
827	Egbert becomes overlord of most of Angle-Lande
838	Danes continue harrasment
868	Aethelred and Alfred (sons of Aethelwulf) make peace with the Danes. The Danelaw is established
870	The Danes kill Edmund, king of East Anglia
871	Alfred becomes king of Wessex
897	Alfred's fleet becomes master of the English Channel
901	Death of Alfred the Great at Winchester
911	Edward the Elder harries the Danes
925	Athelstan the Golden King
937	Athelstan conquers the Danes at Brunaburgh
940	Edmund becomes king
979	Edward the Martyr is murdered
979	Ethelred the Unready becomes king

1002	Ethelred marries Emma of Normandy
	Ethelred precipitates massacre of Danes on St Brice's day
1006	The Danes overrun England
1013	Ethelred flees to Normandy
	Sweyn becomes king of England
1014	Death of Sweyn, Ethelred returns with Edmund
1015	Canute, king of Denmark lands in England
1016	Ethelred dies, Edmund Ironside becomes king
1017	Edmund dies. Canute becomes king. Marries Emma of Normandy.
1035	Death of Canute. Sons Harold and Harthacanute share the rule of England.
1040	Harthacanute becomes sole ruler
1042	Harthacanute dies, Edward son of Ethelred (Unready) and
	Emma succeeds him. Edward marries Edith, daughter of Earl Godwine
1049	Edward the Confessor commences building Westminster Abbey
1064	Harold Godwinesson a guest of Duke William of Normandy
1066	Harald Hardraada of Norway plans invasion of England
	William of Normandy plans invasion of England
	Battle of Stamford Bridge, Harold Victorious
	Battle of Hastings, William Victorious

* * *

GOOD WALKING
BOOKS

goodwalking@aol.com

"it is good to collect things,
but it is better to go on walks."
Bruce Chatwin

redbanana

www.redbanana.com.au